Weightless: Flying Free

Soaring Above Food Issues

Joni Jones

WESTBOW
PRESS®
A DIVISION OF THOMAS NELSON
& ZONDERVAN

Copyright © 2015 Joni Jones.

All rights reserved. No part of this book may be used or reproduced by any means, graphic, electronic, or mechanical, including photocopying, recording, taping or by any information storage retrieval system without the written permission of the author except in the case of brief quotations embodied in critical articles and reviews.

Scriptures taken from the Holy Bible, New International Version®, NIV®. Copyright © 1973, 1978, 1984, 2011 by Biblica, Inc.™ Used by permission of Zondervan. All rights reserved worldwide. www.zondervan.com The "NIV" and "New International Version" are trademarks registered in the United States Patent and Trademark Office by Biblica, Inc.™

WestBow Press books may be ordered through booksellers or by contacting:

WestBow Press
A Division of Thomas Nelson & Zondervan
1663 Liberty Drive
Bloomington, IN 47403
www.westbowpress.com
1 (866) 928-1240

Because of the dynamic nature of the Internet, any web addresses or links contained in this book may have changed since publication and may no longer be valid. The views expressed in this work are solely those of the author and do not necessarily reflect the views of the publisher, and the publisher hereby disclaims any responsibility for them.

Any people depicted in stock imagery provided by Thinkstock are models, and such images are being used for illustrative purposes only.
Certain stock imagery © Thinkstock.

ISBN: 978-1-4908-9815-5 (sc)
ISBN: 978-1-4908-9816-2 (e)

Print information available on the last page.

WestBow Press rev. date: 11/18/2015

Contents

Introduction xiii
Joni's Story 1
Week 1: You Are Not Alone 12
Week 2: Trusting the One Who Heals 17
Week 3: I Like Me: Finding Your Value In God 31
Week 4: God Is My Stronghold 49
Week 5: Putting A Face On The Food Stronghold 66
Week 6: The Promises And Lies of Food 82
Week 7: I Do Have A Choice 97
Week 8: Responding As A Child Of God 118
Week 9: Falling Backwards 135
Week 10: Moving Forward: Flying Wounded Above 152
Week 11: Weightless: Flying Free 167
Week 12: Perfect Peace To Soar 182
Appendix A: Food Diary 189
Appendix B: Additional Resources/Support 191
    BIBLE STUDIES 191
    BOOKS 191
    Weight and Self-Image 191
    Anorexia, Bulimia, Overeaters 192
    Other Issues 192
    WEBSITES 192
ORGANIZATIONS 193
References 195

"Joni Jones has developed a highly effective workbook for recovering from an eating disorder. She provides insights and direction on tough issues through her own recovery story and reflection exercises. She has a gift for spiritual integration, weaving true Christian principles with her practical helps for the reader."

–Eileen Adams, MS,
Professional Relations at
Remuda Ranch Programs for Eating Disorders

"Joni Jones' story is a powerful testimony to a loving and faithful God. In her book, *Weightless: Flying Free,* Joni not only shares her struggles by sharing her heart, she points to The One who healed her. Readers who use this workbook will discover that if we are not consumed by God, we will be consumed by something else. Joni asks the tough questions helping the reader to embrace truth and step out of denial. As one participant in a group I led pointed out, "God is far more concerned with my wounds than my waist."

–Judy Webb
Director of Small Groups
The Church at Mill Run

To my husband Hoyt...
For loving me through "thick and thin" with his Christ-like heart

Flying Free

The bulimia I so hated, as I struggled from day to day–
The bondage that I was in, I thought was the only way.
I wanted it to vanish, yet I held with all my might–
On the quest for perfection, it was what I thought was right.

Managing my disorder, became a way of life–
It was part of my identity, as I was a mother and a wife.
Who would I be without it, how would I ever be able to cope–
With pain, rejection, loneliness, I truly didn't see any hope.

So I held on tightly to this monster, disguised as my best friend–
Daily destroying my body and mind, how else was I to mend.
When desperate I became, I just wanted it to be gone–
I cried out to God and accepted, Jesus His beloved Son.

He is the key to the freedom; He restored my past life of pain–
To God I give the glory, in my life He will always reign!

Introduction

This is a book about God's amazing power; what He has done in my life and what He can do in yours. I am blown away by the love of God. He took me, His damaged daughter, and cared for, loved, and bandaged me back to wholeness. When I was suffering all alone in pain…God was there. When no one would listen to me…God was there. When I felt unloved…God was there. When I cried…God was there. When I felt I just couldn't go on…God was there. God was there, even when I didn't feel Him. He was patient with me in my impatience. He wiped my tears through it all.

I am not a therapist or doctor. I am just an ordinary person who lived through a food stronghold for 14 years and now is healed. I know the pain; I know how hard the struggle. I understand when you look in the mirror and all you see is "fat," and "thin" is never thin enough. I understand the pain of "feeling fat." I understand how food can control you. I understand the desire to want the food stronghold to be gone…yet you remain stuck. I understand the pain of wanting something so bad, or hating it so much, yet being unable to let it go.

Dear one, I know the struggle you face is hard and painful. I know the hurt. I know the hopelessness. I fought the fight, and I couldn't have done it without God. God is the reason that I am alive today to share His message, to share His power, to share His hope with all of you. My battle with food issues is over. There are many more battles to face in this world, but with God on and at my side, I don't fear any longer. I persevere because He gives me strength. I trust because He can be trusted. I choose to believe when doubt comes my way. I have been freed from the clutches of this horrible battle. I've experienced the healing power of Jesus Christ. He is the Way, the Truth, and the Life.

> Dear one, I know the struggle you face is hard and painful. I know the hurt. I know the hopelessness.

He is bigger than the food stronghold in your life now. He wants to deliver you from it. It doesn't matter how long you have suffered in your stronghold, as God is faithful and restores. You just have to take His hand and begin the journey, which you will never forget. I pray that God will fill you with His hope as you take this road to recovery. He will not leave your side…no matter what. It's worth the journey.

***As you begin to face your food stronghold and "get to the heart of what is eating you", it is natural to cling to the stronghold more, since it has served a role in your life. Rest assured, while you continue to work through this workbook. Try not to get discouraged, for the Lord God is with you wherever you go. Give yourself grace and accept God's grace.

Over the next twelve weeks you will be discovering what lies beneath the food stronghold in your life. A food stronghold is a symptom of emotions and hurts. This workbook is merely a tool and not the answer; the true answer lies in your relationship with God. Whether you are completing this workbook in a group setting or by yourself, I recommend you to surround yourself with those who will be an encouragement to you.

If you are struggling with anorexia or bulimia, it is essential to see a doctor and/or a therapist. This book should not be a substitute for the medical attention that you may need.

Defining a stronghold:

Food Stronghold: I would prefer to use the words "food stronghold" or "eating behavior" when referencing your struggle with anorexia, bulimia, or compulsive overeating. I believe that this is a stronghold in your life that Jesus Christ is able to free you from. This stronghold which you are suffering from is not who you are. A stronghold is "anything that exalts itself in our minds, pretending to be bigger or more powerful than our God. It steals our focus and causes us to feel overpowered. Controlled. Mastered. …it consumes so much of our emotional and mental energy that it strangles our abundant life" (Moore, 10). This describes the effects of anorexia, bulimia, and compulsive overeating in one's life.

> **If you are struggling with anorexia or bulimia, it is essential to see a doctor and/or a therapist. This book should not be a substitute for the medical attention that you may need.**

Food as a Drug

Food, the source of nourishment, has become the drug of choice for many. It is an acceptable "drug," because food is needed to survive. When did this source of nourishment turn into such a monster destroying the lives of women, men, teens, and children? It begins as an innocent form of weight control or coping mechanism, which eventually grows into a life threatening way of life. The National Association of Anorexia Nervosa and Associated Disorders states that approximately 8 million people in the United States suffer from anorexia nervosa, bulimia, and other related eating behaviors. They conclude that about 3 out of every 100 people are plagued with the abuse of food in a way that is detrimental to their health. It is hard to get an accurate account since medical professionals are not required to report food related issues and that most individuals practice the behavior in secret (ANRED).

What is an eating disorder (food stronghold)? It is a medical condition that involves disturbance to the normal functioning of the mind or body through the abuse of food (Encarta). It is self-destructive behavior, involving guilt and fear, leading to denial (Vath, 31). It is a behavior that you control, yet it controls your life. The term "closet eater" or "the hidden disease" describes most disordered eating patterns. "Eating Disorders" is a general term which describes many different relationships one has with food. Bulimia, anorexia nervosa, and compulsive eating, are the predominant labels given to the abuse of food and the body. Besides the most common forms of eating disorders, 15% of young women have issues with food (Claude-Pierre).

Anorexia Nervosa is "the relentless pursuit of thinness and an attempt to maintain control over food intake" (C.C.E.D.). The main characteristics are "...preoccupation with body weight, behaviors directed toward losing weight, and intense fear of gaining weight, coupled with an unusual preoccupation with food including bizarre behaviors in handling it" (Vath, 37). There is a fear of losing control. An anorexic weight is usually 85% or less of what it should be for his/her weight and height. Starvation, obsessive exercising,

> An eating disorder is a medical condition which involves disturbance to the normal functioning of the mind or body through the abuse of food.

calorie/fat counting, use of pills/laxatives/diuretics to control weight, and hiding and throwing away food are some of the most prevalent behavioral signs. In addition to weight loss, other physical symptoms that may occur are the loss of menstruation in women, hair loss, dizziness, headaches, low blood pressure, depression, fatigue and insomnia, and often feeling cold.

Bulimia is the food behavior that is characterized by "...recurrent, compulsive episodes of binge eating (rapid consumption of a large amount of food in a short period of time), followed by self-induced vomiting and/or purging with laxatives and/or diuretics" (Vath, 37). Other behavioral symptoms may include hiding and stealing of food, and dieting. Bulimia is a "hidden" disease. Most bulimics are able to assume what appears to be a normal lifestyle. Like anorexia, it isolates a person. The bulimic bases his/her self-worth on being thin. Physical symptoms that the bulimic may experience are low potassium levels causing dehydration, damage to the heart, kidney and brain, ruptured esophagus, stomach disorders, acid reflux, teeth erosion, and fluctuations of weight.

Compulsive overeating, or binge eating disorder, is characterized by "periods of impulsive gorging or continuous eating (C.C.E.D). Compulsive overeaters usually do not purge, obsessively exercise, or abuse laxatives. Their genetic make-up may be more susceptible to weight gain, which may lead to yo-yo dieting. Diets usually will lead to a binge in response to the hunger produced from the food denied during dieting. An addiction to food is usually a prevalent behavioral sign used to fill an emotional void.

Food strongholds are not about the food. The food is used as a numbing agent or a form of control in response to underlying issues. The most common factor is one of self-esteem. A disorder usually begins with a change in eating patterns for the purpose of coping or weight control, but if one's not careful, it will usually turn into a food stronghold. Societal messages about the body and weight feed the eating behavior. The messages of eating more, coupled with diets and exercise to get the perfect body, are sending mixed messages. Some other factors that may be contributors are body dissatisfaction,

> Food strongholds are not about the food. The food is used as a numbing agent or a form of control in response to underlying issues. The most common factor is one of self-esteem.

self-esteem issues, depression, perfectionism, physical, emotional or sexual abuse, and comments about one's size and weight.

There are stages that lead to a food stronghold. As God uncovered the emotions and the purpose of the eating behaviors in my life, I saw a progression that took place. I observed this same progression in the lives of others who struggle with various food strongholds. The stages leading to the development of a food stronghold (progression) can be described like a balloon. A deflated balloon is the individual at birth. A triggering event starts the process. The reaction is in the form of using food in an unhealthy manner (binging/dieting/starving) or some other obsessive behavior, which adds some air into the balloon. More air is added each time the person adds another controlling behavior after a triggering event. As your life becomes consumed with managing the behavior, the balloon keeps inflating…eventually causing the balloon to pop. This is the point of desperation. The once innocent diet has now become a food stronghold that consumes your life. You have reached the end of your rope and realize that you have a problem. The opportunity to change and begin recovery is at this point; the point where some may reach for God and begin the recovery process. The secret in the recovery is the healing of the pain caused by the initial triggering event. Jesus is the only one who has the power to heal this pain, as He has done in my life. The progression is outlined by the following seven stages:

i. **Triggering Event** which leads to some form of obsessive behavior
ii. **Obsessive behaviors begin** (coping mechanism, such as nail biting, picking at oneself, fear, performance behaviors…may be subtle)
iii. **Behavior modification** (dieting, starving, exercising)
iv. **Triggering Event** - pushing the intensity of the behavior (an innocent diet or exercise program becomes anorexia, bulimia)
v. **Obsessed with new behavior** (gaining recognition through weight loss, therefore becoming the individual's way of life, a means to the end of achieving perfection)

vi. **Realization there is a problem, desperate state**
vii. **Choice to change**: Recovery Process

Food strongholds are very complex since they involve every aspect of a person: physical, mental, emotional, and spiritual. All of these areas have to be examined, with the spiritual becoming part of all of them. The key to complete recovery from any type of eating disorder is to identify and heal the underlying issues which fuel the behavior, which in turn will help to restore a healthy relationship with food, producing a healthy body. This can be achieved through therapy, nutritional counseling, and most importantly having God as the center of your life.

Complete recovery is possible, as I am a walking testimony of the power of God. God is the food for the heart, mind, and body. When God is the center of your life, true healing and freedom will be found. He supplies you physically with His strength, mentally with the renewing of your mind, emotionally with His unconditional love, and spiritually with His Son, Jesus Christ who provides true freedom. God gives you the feet to stand on as you begin to shed the powerful monsters of anorexia, bulimia, and compulsive overeating.

> **Food strongholds are very complex since they involve every aspect of a person: physical, mental, emotional, and spiritual.**

Do You Suffer from an Eating Disorder (Food Stronghold)?

The following list contains behavior patterns that reflect those of an eating disorder. Check each question that is true in your life (past or present).

__1. Do thoughts about food occupy much of your time?
__2. Are you preoccupied with a desire to be thinner?
__3. Do you starve to make up for eating binges?
__4. Are you overweight despite concern by others for you to lose weight?
__5. Do you binge and then purge afterward?
__6. Do you exercise excessively to burn off calories?
__7. Do you overeat by binging or by grazing continuously?
__8. Do you eat the same thing every day and feel annoyed when you eat something else?

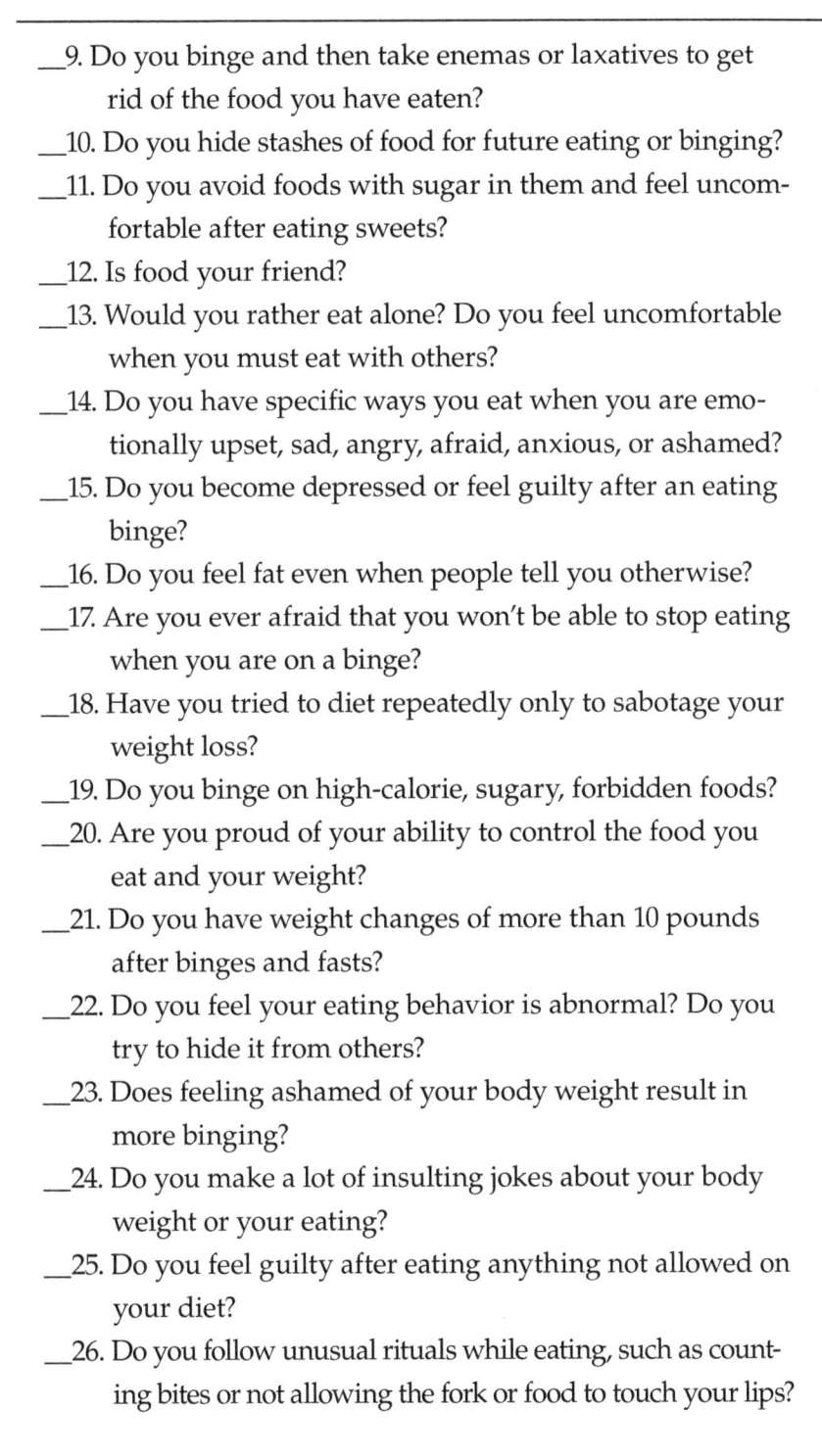

__9. Do you binge and then take enemas or laxatives to get rid of the food you have eaten?
__10. Do you hide stashes of food for future eating or binging?
__11. Do you avoid foods with sugar in them and feel uncomfortable after eating sweets?
__12. Is food your friend?
__13. Would you rather eat alone? Do you feel uncomfortable when you must eat with others?
__14. Do you have specific ways you eat when you are emotionally upset, sad, angry, afraid, anxious, or ashamed?
__15. Do you become depressed or feel guilty after an eating binge?
__16. Do you feel fat even when people tell you otherwise?
__17. Are you ever afraid that you won't be able to stop eating when you are on a binge?
__18. Have you tried to diet repeatedly only to sabotage your weight loss?
__19. Do you binge on high-calorie, sugary, forbidden foods?
__20. Are you proud of your ability to control the food you eat and your weight?
__21. Do you have weight changes of more than 10 pounds after binges and fasts?
__22. Do you feel your eating behavior is abnormal? Do you try to hide it from others?
__23. Does feeling ashamed of your body weight result in more binging?
__24. Do you make a lot of insulting jokes about your body weight or your eating?
__25. Do you feel guilty after eating anything not allowed on your diet?
__26. Do you follow unusual rituals while eating, such as counting bites or not allowing the fork or food to touch your lips?

If you checked five or more of the questions numbered 1, 4, 7, 12, 13, 14, 15, 17, 18, 19, 22, 23, 24, you may be dealing with compulsive overeating.

If you checked five or more of the questions numbered 1, 2, 6, 8, 11, 13, 14, 16, 17, 20, 22, 25, 26, you have eating behaviors typical of anorexia nervosa.

If you checked five or more of the questions numbered 1, 3, 5, 6, 9, 10, 13, 14, 15, 17, 19, 21, 22, 26, you have eating behaviors common in bulimia nervosa. (Celebrate Recovery)

Take heart if you discovered that you have an issue with food. Acknowledgement is the first step to recovery. There is hope for you as you take the Lord's hand to lead you on a journey that will produce a life of freedom.

Joni's Story

"Come and listen, all you who fear God;
  let me tell you what He has done for me.
I cried out to Him with my mouth;
  His praise was on my tongue.
If I had cherished sin in my heart,
  the Lord would not have listened;
but God has surely listened
  and heard my voice in prayer.
Praise be to God,
  who has not rejected my prayer
or withheld His love from me!"

—Psalm 66:16-20

Psalm 66:16-20 describes the beginning of my road to recovery from food strongholds. Ever since that first cry out to the Lord, my life has not been the same. It is a cry that saved my life, and I pray that it is a cry that will save your life as well.

Food Gone Sour

Why food? Why did I begin to abuse something that I loved? My love of food began as a child. Food was associated with happy times. It was always the focus at all family gatherings. Food was used as a reward. It provided the solution to everything. Food became synonymous with good, happy, fun, and most importantly love. I also received a lot of mixed messages about eating. Meal times were times of eating as much as you wanted, yet "treats" were strictly regulated. What started as something positive, later led to my destruction.

> Why food? Why did I begin to abuse something that I loved?

As I was growing up and negative emotions would emerge, subconsciously I would want the "good" feeling, so I turned to food. Food became a mask over those negative emotions. When food wasn't available, I would have to "pick" at something else. The picking spread over to critical thinking and the picking of my nails, fingers, and toes until they bled. My quest to relieve the pain, instead intensified it. At the time, I did not see anything wrong with the behavior.

Birth of the Food Stronghold

I began to diet in 5th grade. I was not overweight. A family friend had made a comment that I was getting "fat." At that time, all the critical comments and teasing about my appearance, my body shape, and my desires, overpowered my mind. This confirmed to me that being me was not enough, therefore triggering me into my quest for perfection.

Never Enough

I internalized every word and action to mean that there was something wrong with me. I felt a constant pressure and battle, as who God made me to be was in opposition to who others said I should be. Confusion set in; if what I felt or what I liked to do was criticized, then that meant that there must be something wrong with me. Every time I would just *be*, I would get stripped of it. I just wasn't allowed to be who God created me to be. I was being molded into someone else. Who did they want me to be? What is wrong with me as I am?

I began searching for an identity through performance, since I believed that my own identity was not good enough. I tried to be the perfect child. I became a neat freak. My bedroom was always perfect, yet that didn't seem enough. I helped around the house, but it was never enough. I tried to be the smart one, but never smart enough. I tried to be the pretty one, but there was always a flaw. So...I decided to become the thin one....

Damaged Freight

During my recovery, through a journaling time with God, I learned that my pain began before that first diet at the age of eleven. That diet was the triggering event that set the ball in motion. I had a deep open cut, a wound that needed to be filled. I was starving for attention as a child. At 14 months old, I almost died of dehydration. It was a horrible time for my parents, which brought them great pain. Whenever this event was referenced, I deducted that it was my fault that it happened, and that I had caused my parents pain. This incident fueled the lie that I had to be punished for being who I was and that I was not enough. I became damaged freight, therefore I deserved to be treated as so. Unless the original wound or hurt is healed, the present and future will be infected by its pain.

Stuffed Emotions

I became preoccupied with my appearance...what I wore, hiding my body in big clothes, and consumed with my weight. My first "innocent diet" turned into a battle. I truly believed that it was all about the weight, but today I realize that it was just a bandage I wore over my stuffed emotions.

I began to control the one thing that I loved and what I thought was love...food. What I was raised with that meant love and happiness, started to cause me pain...weight gain. I began to associate "fat" with bad. Food was no longer a means of nutrition. I began my love/hate relationship with food, which continued into my college years and beyond.

The pressures of always dieting and denying myself led me into "sneaking" food. Since I wasn't good enough to have the food, then I would have to "sneak it." I began secretly binging on food. I would then have to punish myself the next day by starving or exercising obsessively to purge the food from my body. A cycle began that wouldn't stop. I was subconsciously cheating on my own rules that I set up, because I still needed the food for comfort. What game was I playing?

> I became preoccupied with my appearance... what I wore, hiding my body in big clothes, and consumed with my weight. My first "innocent diet" turned into a battle.

Searching...

In high school I became more self-conscious. Days after a binge, I wouldn't go to school because I felt "fat" and couldn't find anything to wear...still not good enough. I was so consumed by how I looked that it was stealing any possible joy that I could have. I was living a double life...who was I? I was getting tired of the dieting and the pain that I carried around.

Something was telling me that there was something more to life than trying to be a certain weight or size. I believe God began to churn in my heart, revealing that it was Him that I needed. I began reading self-help books. I began to listen more intently to the sermons in church. Throughout my childhood I went to church. I grew up with very strong morals and values. I believed in God, but a God whom I feared. I knew He was watching me, so I had to be careful about my actions. I grew up with a religion of good and bad, dos and don'ts. I was actually afraid of the Bible because I didn't want to become the stereotypic religious freak. I had my God on Sundays, and He was always in the back of my mind, and I thought that was enough. The seeds were being planted.

Discovery of Bulimia

College, I thought, was the answer to my pain. It was my new-found freedom to do what I wanted to do when I wanted to do it, and not be judged. And another freedom, freedom with food.

My roommate and I learned of the freedom of eating anything we wanted, especially all of those forbidden foods. We would then go on crazy starvation diets. I then became more obsessive about dieting, especially since I had met my future husband, Hoyt that year, and I had to look good. I was truly in love. I became Hoyt's girlfriend; this had to be enough. I began to perform again, even though Hoyt liked me for who I was. I was afraid to be just me. I had to keep him. No one was going to take him away.

My sophomore year in college was a turning point for me. Hoyt had graduated, and our long distance relationship had begun. I was very lonely. He was in my heart, but gone. What did I have now?

After one too many binges, and feeling quite sick, a friend made the suggestion of purging the food. I took the "advice." I discovered bulimia. Yes! I thought I had just found the key to life. I would never have to diet again. It was fun. I could take this wherever I went. No one could take that away. I became Joni the bulimic. When I was alone I could go to food and eat everything I wanted to and then purge. What a relief. If someone hurt me, I could use food again. If I was afraid, I was safe because I had my friend who would never leave me...bulimia. I found my purpose. I found Joni.

Living the Lie

Not only did I use food for the comfort it provided, I planned binges and the places where I would purge. I found nothing wrong with it. It was my hidden secret...hidden because I did not want anyone to take it from me. I would deny anything if accused. I was the master.

I filled up on the stronghold day and night. I would eat those forbidden foods of my childhood, massive quantities and then purge. "My" bulimia became a way of life for me. I had it down to a science. I thought I found the answer of "having my cake and eating it too." It was a challenge. My every minute was consumed with what my next binge was going to be and where I could purge. I had to plan it right, because I didn't want to get caught. No one could find out. I feared someone taking it away from me. This was mine. This was my protective coat against the world.

Each time I filled up on this, I lost a part of the true Joni. I was living a life of denial. What I thought was my friend, my identity, was actually my enemy. I poured my life into it. I appeared to have it all together and that I could achieve perfection this way. I performed to whoever wanted a performance. I was great...and if I wasn't great, I still had the bulimia. I found the key to life. Now no one could hurt me anymore. No one could steal who I was. I had the power. I had it all... so I thought. I continued the behavior throughout my college years.... But now, the bulimia was beginning to become a problem.

> **What I thought was my friend, my identity, was actually my enemy.**

Moving on

The high point of my life came when my husband asked me to become his wife the summer before my senior year. A dream too good to be true. What could be better than being in love and getting married? Now that I was marrying my true love, there was no more room for bulimia. Well, I still continued the bulimia, especially because I had to be a skinny bride, but after the wedding I knew I would stop.

I was married and off to graduate school with my new husband. Bulimia was behind me, so I thought. New pressures entered my life…moving away from home, being a wife, starting graduate school, and teaching. I needed my old friend, bulimia, to cope. I kept this hidden from my husband.

Well, I thought my cure came…again. I found out I was pregnant. This was the answer. Bulimia wasn't an option any longer. I did not purge throughout my pregnancy. I felt so free. We were blessed with our precious daughter. But the postpartum stage of pregnancy set me back into the bulimia. I truly believed that I would never do it again. I couldn't deal with the extra weight, so I began the binge/purge cycle…again. I was truly happy and so blessed to have a family, so why would I even consider it? After looking into the eyes of my precious daughter, I made a promise to stop the bulimia, because I did not want her or my husband to ever suffer because of my choice. It wasn't their fault, it was my issue.

I graduated from grad school and the food stronghold was in full swing. The adjustment to living away from my family, married, and now being a new mom and not having school to fall back on, pushed every one of my buttons. I basically dealt with life by eating and purging. It was at this point that I realized this was more than just a weight thing.

We moved to another state, where I then became pregnant with my wonderful son. Again, I thought this was the answer to the bulimia, but it came back with a vengeance. After I delivered my precious son, I felt great. I only had five pounds to lose and I could fit into my clothes. This didn't matter, because I still continued in the binging and purging…along with breastfeeding and running. This lasted for about six weeks and then I almost passed out. I went into a deep depression and blamed it on postpartum. I didn't even tell my gynecologist. The bulimia was becoming a burden that would eventually infect my family. God is the only one who kept me alive at that time. I had to rid myself of this horrible monster because of my family.

Our family was off to a different state and this is where I finally confronted my husband about the bulimia. Thanks to him, he found help for me. I met with a nutritionist, and learned how to eat nutritionally. I stopped purging, but became compulsive about my eating. My nutritionist suggested I see a therapist, but I refused. I felt if my eating was under control, then the bulimia was too.

Another move, another state.... Every time we moved I would make a promise to myself that I would not purge in our new toilet. Well, the stronghold followed me. I decided to see a nutritionist again because it was less threatening than a therapist, and all I thought I needed was someone to strictly monitor my food. I began charting my food again, compulsively and even started doing a liquid diet. I started the bulimic behavior after the pressure of a trip home to see my family and wanting to look and be perfect. It was at that point that I finally called a therapist.

I discovered that I had a lot of issues that were hiding behind the food stronghold. It just wasn't my desire to be thin. It wasn't about the food. The bulimia was just the by-product. Therapy helped me to uncover the many layers that were fueling this disorder…perfectionism, low self-esteem, black and white thinking, rejection issues, …. Awareness was the first step. I had hope. I then became pregnant with my third child. I again thought this was a cure, sent from God. After I gave birth to another precious gift, a daughter, I fell back into the bulimia. I found another therapist and a support group. I attended therapy twice a week and worked really hard. I got involved in a church and felt closer to God. I read many books on food strongholds and was in the healing process. The bulimic behavior continued, but I was beginning to recognize the triggers that would send me into the disorder. I finally had turned a corner, and I learned how to "manage" the bulimia. Later, I discovered that managing the behavior meant that it was still alive in me waiting to emerge. I was bulimia free for

> I discovered that I had a lot of issues that were hiding behind the food stronghold. It just wasn't my desire to be thin.

about 6 months…and then we moved again (my freedom was also due to the fact that my husband was handling everything that would trigger me).

I was excited because I hadn't binged or purged, and felt I was finally free. Well, I blew my "I am not going to throw up in our new toilet" goal. The stresses of moving and starting all over again pushed me over the edge, making food and the bulimic behavior my best friend.

A Cry For Help

The binge purge cycle continued. At this point, I was concerned about my health. The "high" that I used to experience after a binge and purge, diminished. I now felt worse after a binge purge cycle. I couldn't sleep at night. I was full of fear…fear of dying. My heart would race until I would break out into a cold sweat. I believed I was going to have a heart attack because of what I was doing to my body. I would "swear" not to do it again. Who would take care of my kids and my husband if I were gone? How selfish of me to be so irresponsible. When I would get up the next morning, so thankful that I was alive, I would have a new lease on life. Within hours, the bulimic behavior continued. I was back in the cycle. I was hooked. I thought I controlled this stronghold, when in turn it controlled me. I lost all hope. I knew that I was always going to be "Joni the bulimic."

I felt like a shell. The bulimia that I used to fill me was instead emptying me. I really felt like I was not enough. There was something missing. I, in my own power, was working too hard and not getting anywhere. I was just controlling a behavior that was destroying me instead of providing me with what I though it was intended to.

It was bigger than I was and out of my control. I realized that I needed more than a nutritionist and a therapist to get rid of this horrible monster. A stirring in my heart told me that I needed God. I carried around the God of my youth. I talked to Him, but He wasn't in my heart. I strongly believed He existed, but I really didn't know Him. As I look back over my life, I see how God was constantly trying to get my attention, yet I pushed Him aside. There was always a Christian in my life, from my friend in high school, to my college roommate, to

> **It was bigger than I was and out of my control. I realized that I needed more than a nutritionist and a therapist to get rid of this horrible monster.**

friends in every state I lived, but I never thought twice about it because I believed I was a Christian too. My aunt and her family became Christians, and I used to laugh when I heard that they were praying for me, even before the bulimia. Well, those prayers were needed now.

In desperation, I called my aunt and asked her what I had to do to find God, because I needed Him. She lovingly found me a Christian church in my area. Little did I know that their prayers were finally about to be answered.

Hope

Fearfully, one Sunday, I sought out the church. Totally opposite of the church I attended as a child, I thought, *How could this be church?* The music began. People clapped, people cried, people smiled. Emotions in church, happiness in church, why all the tears? It just happened to be a baptismal Sunday, so testimonies were being read. The honesty of their struggles, addictions, the transforming power of God. Wow, God can really change people. I left there confused, yet hopeful.

I returned the following week and my heart opened up. This was the turning point in my life. I attended the service and couldn't stop crying...real tears over the hurts and the emptiness of the past. I could feel the pain that I was hiding for so many years. I also felt the joy around me. Something was different about "their" God. The sermon blew me away. I never knew that what the pastor was speaking about was in the Bible. Actually, I didn't even know what was in the Bible. I didn't know that I needed the forgiveness that only Jesus offers. I walked out in a trance. Something was happening to me. I felt peace for the first time in my life. I found God.

My Hope in Recovery

The door of my heart was opened when I gave it to my Lord. Jesus came in and began the healing process. I couldn't get enough of God. I spent hours in the Bible getting to know my Lord. As I grew in my faith, I was able to shed the shackles from the past. I had a lot of baggage, but it wasn't too much for God. He began to heal those wounds of the past that I carried with me into adulthood. He never gave up on me, even when I wanted to.

God is faithful. God has given me a second, third, fourth... chance. He has blessed me with three children and a husband. He has placed the most loving women of God in my life to provide the support I needed along the way. All because He loves me. He never stopped loving me, even when I was in the trenches of the bulimia. I finally found the key that I was looking for. Full recovery became a reality.

I allowed my God to start putting Joni back together. God began to put me back together piece by piece. Painful at times, but always worth it. I finally took His hand and I will never let it go.

The Truth

The bulimia was a lie. I allowed this lie to steal many precious years from me. I was born to be Joni, but not allowed to be. I felt naked. All alone. Empty. It was then that God came. He began to fill my emptiness. God glued me back together. God healed me. Today, I know who Joni is. I know what Joni likes and dislikes. I know what angers and frustrates Joni. I know what makes Joni laugh. I know what brings joy to Joni. I know what Joni likes to eat. I know what makes Joni feel good. I know Joni's boundaries. I am finally becoming the Joni that God created.

In my quest for perfection, I was looking in the wrong direction and was blinded. I kept striving to attain it in the perfect weight, size, and appearance. How unrealistic. What is perfect? ...it doesn't exist. When I would reach what I thought was perfect, it wasn't perfect enough. I was trying to achieve the unachievable. Satan led me to believe I could achieve it if only I tried harder, dieted more, purged more, and exercised... more. The answer was in my heart, and that is what God wanted. Today I am perfect, perfect in Christ, and this is a perfection that will last into eternity.

I continue to grow in the Lord and have Him fill those empty hurt spots in my life...because He is the only one that can. I thirst for my God because He thirsts for me first. Do I regret the past? No, because it is what brought me to my knees. God has restored all those years. He has restored the years the locusts have eaten (Joel 2:25).

> **The bulimia was a lie. I allowed this lie to steal many precious years from me. I was born to be Joni, but not allowed to be.**

Joy through the pain

The story of my struggle with bulimia and the inner pain I carried is just a part of my story. I have shared the painful times, the painful inner battles I experienced inside of me. I felt like I had two sides to me: the bulimic, hurting Joni that I tried so hard to never let interfere with my family, and the Joni, wife and mother, who just loved and truly enjoyed every minute of her children's and husband's lives. The other part of the story is beautiful. Through all of this I was able to truly enjoy and love my children and my husband. Those years are precious and the memories just make me cry tears of joy. As I look back over my life, I just smile. To just wake up and see their precious faces in the morning, gave me a reason to live life to the full. It was my love for them that kept me going. The pain of the bulimic years and their memories are never in the same thought. I am very blessed that the food stronghold never robbed my family. I thank the Lord for the precious gifts of my children, and my loving husband who has shown me the meaning of God's unconditional love by supporting me and, most especially, by loving me as I am. To God, I give all the thanks and the glory!

Week 1

You Are Not Alone

> *"Have I not commanded you? Be strong and courageous.
> Do not be terrified; do not be discouraged, for the Lord
> your God will be with you wherever you go."*
> Joshua 1:9

Welcome and Purpose

Welcome to the beginning of a new life — a new start. I praise you for your strength and courage and for taking the first step to freedom from the food stronghold that grips you. You will find freedom as you begin to trust the Lord, who heals, restores, and loves you. You are not alone in this. This will be a worthwhile experience as you allow God to free you. I know this to be true, because I have lived it. I pray that you will experience God's love and peace as you embrace Him as your own.

> *"Let us hold unswervingly to the hope we profess, for He who
> promised is faithful. And let us consider how we may spur one
> another on toward love and good deeds. Let us not give up meeting
> together, as some are in the habit of doing, but let us encourage
> one another—and all the more as you see the Day approaching."*
> Hebrews 10:23-25

Opening Prayer

Dear Lord, Surround me with Your presence and Your peace as I begin this journey to recovery. Become my safe place—a place of comfort and encouragement where I can openly share my heart. In Jesus' name I pray.

Opening Your Heart

1. What are your expectations from this study?

   _____

   _____

   _____

2. Note any help (programs, therapy, diets) that you have received or in which you are currently involved. What has provided change?

   _____

   _____

   _____

3. Where do you find encouragement?

   _____

   _____

   _____

4. What/who encourages you the most? Why?

   _____

   _____

   _____

"Therefore confess your sins to each other and pray for each other so that you may be healed. The prayer of a righteous man is powerful and effective."—James 5:16

14 / *Weightless: Flying Free*

> "Therefore confess your sins to each other and pray for each other so that you may be healed. The prayer of a righteous man is powerful and effective."
> —James 5:16

5. Referring to James 5:16, what is an essential part of your recovery?

   _____
   _____
   _____

6. How do you feel as you begin this journey to freedom?

   _____
   _____
   _____

7. Write a prayer, asking the Lord for what you need as you begin the recovery process.

   _____
   _____
   _____

A life without anorexia, bulimia, and compulsive overeating is really possible—but for you? The answer is *yes!* Christ has freed me, and He is able to set you free, too. Stop making this a dream and an "if only" in your life. Make this reality. Christ has come to set us free (John 8:32), and you are no exception. I truly believed that healing was for someone else and not for me. I didn't believe that I deserved this freedom. I couldn't even imagine my life without my good buddy bulimia. It became who I was. It was me, and I thought it would always be me.

8. What are the first words that come to mind when you hear the words *food* and *diet*?

   _____
   _____
   _____

9. How would you describe your relationship with food? Is food your friend, foe, or both? Why?

_____

_____

_____

10. Do you believe you are in control of food, or is food in control of you?

_____

_____

_____

11. Picture yourself without a food stronghold. How do you see yourself? What feelings/emotions do you experience when you envision this?

_____

_____

_____

12. What hope does Joshua 1:9 offer you?

_____

_____

_____

The recovery process is just that—a process of healing. Every process will look different, so try not to compare. God will reveal emotions and feelings that have been masked by a food stronghold. You are beginning a time of self-discovery. Feelings may be intense, but they will not destroy. Trust God with the process.

My prayer for you is to surround yourself with encouragers who provide a safe place for you to share your heart and to find comfort. Most importantly, you must make God your safe place, as He is the key to helping you move beyond the food stronghold in your life. Be proud that you have made a decision to be free. Enjoy the ride, and let God take you on a trip you will never forget.

Food for Thought

Brand New

"A new time, a new day, a new year. Maybe this time, dear Lord, a new me. I'll leave behind the old shell of insecurities, and travel the road to wholeness. I'll put my faith in you, Lord, and learn to love this gift of life You've given me" (Remuda Ranch).

"God works through people … The message of Christian Recovery is that God's grace is experienced as a process which involves intensely honest and nurturing relationships with other people. They serve as agents of His grace to unravel our woundedness and reshape our thinking" (Liimatta).

Memory Verse

"Have I not commanded you? Be strong and courageous. Do not be terrified; do not be discouraged, for the Lord your God will be with you wherever you go."
Joshua 1:9

Closing Prayer

Dear Lord, Thank You for being with me through this journey. Open my heart to Your Word as I work through this workbook. Fill me with Your strength and courage as You take me through the healing process to freedom. In Jesus' name I pray.

Flying Forward

- Memorize Joshua 1:9.
- Read through next week's study and complete each day's questions throughout the week.

Week 2

Trusting the One Who Heals

"Even youths grow tired and weary, and young men stumble and fall; but those who hope in the Lord will renew their strength. They will soar on wings like eagles; they will run and not grow weary, they will walk and not be faint."
Isaiah 40:30-31

Opening Prayer

Dear Lord, I need You. I want to know You. Take control of my life. Open up my heart to You and Your Word. Fill me with Your strength and hope as I release this food stronghold to You. Thank You that I am able to open my heart honestly to You about my feelings, mistakes, and sins. In Jesus' name I pray.

Truth

I can trust the One who heals.

> I can trust the One who heals.

Day 1: Hope in the Process

I was terrified to face the fact that the binge/purge cycle that I practiced for over fourteen years actually had a name—bulimia—and was destroying my life. This realization set in when the bulimia controlled me instead of me controlling the bulimia. I thought that bulimia was just a habit and a form of weight control that I could give up when I reached my ideal weight and size—the number that always changed and was never good enough. While running after perfection, I was destroying myself. Was I really running after the weight or the size? What was I really running after?

I did not want to face the truth that something was wrong with my behavior. I didn't want to look behind the mask. The more I denied that I needed help (subconsciously, I knew the truth), the more I clung to the behavior. I immersed myself in binging and purging to cover all the intense emotions that tried to emerge.

The truth that help was necessary became a reality. I had tried it all—diets, excessive exercise, self-help books. I began with a nonthreatening approach by seeing a nutritionist and learned how to eat nutritionally. I stopped purging, but I became compulsive about my eating. After the nutritionist suggested I see a therapist, even though I wasn't purging, I closed the door on getting any more help. I believed that it was all about the food, and if I could control the food, then I could control the purging.

The purging behavior eventually raised its ugly head again, and I knew I needed more than a nutritionist. It was bigger than I was. It was out of my power. I fearfully decided to see a therapist. Therapy began to reveal that the bulimic behavior was not really about food or my desire to be thin. I began to uncover the many layers that were behind the bulimia. Bringing to light my stuffed feelings and issues was very overwhelming. Realizing that I was not a bad or weak person for having a food stronghold was half the battle. How could I ever get over all those hurts, feelings, issues, and emotions that I had stuffed for so long? Having to just face the process that was to begin brought on a slew of new emotions. The process began; yet something was missing. Where was I to find comfort as I exposed my inner self, secrets, thoughts, and feelings?

In my decision to get better, I began a road that was painful at times. Sometimes I felt that I was bleeding with no relief. I was very vulnerable and felt naked. I felt like an open wound to which peroxide was applied. True recovery did not begin until I cried out to the Lord and He came into my life. This was the missing piece—not just the piece, but also the answer. Peroxide that is applied to an open cut may sting, but it does promote healing. Little did I know that the stream of events that began was God's way of leading me into a recovery process of true inner healing and restoration. This process restored what sin took away. In this process of growth and self-discovery, I discovered

> **The truth that help was necessary became a reality. I had tried it all—diets, excessive exercise, self-help books.**

the real me—the me that God made me to be. It was a process that I embraced. With God on my side, I had nothing to fear.

God's promise that "never will I leave you; never will I forsake you" (Hebrews 13:5) became a truth of which I have never let go. He was always there to carry me, hear my cries, comfort me, and just love me as I am. I did not have to fear as the roots to the bulimia were uncovered, because God was with me—always—no matter what.

> God's promise that "never will I leave you; never will I forsake you" (Hebrews 13:5) became a truth of which I have never let go.

1. What is your food stronghold? Are your days controlled by the behavior?

   _____
   _____
   _____

2. Do you have any fears as you face giving up your stronghold? If so, what are they?

   _____
   _____
   _____

3. According to Romans 15:13, who supplies hope? What do you need to do in order to receive that hope?

   _____
   _____
   _____

4. Are you willing and ready to allow God to change you from the inside out? Explain.

   _____
   _____
   _____

5. Read Isaiah 43:2-3. Where will God be as you go through this process of recovery? How does that make you feel?

_____

_____

_____

Day 2: Resting in the Arms of the One Who Cares

I was restless, restless every day…always running, but running in the wrong direction, to the wrong things. I thought I held the key to life…food. It was my protector, my friend. It calmed me. It was always available. It was my refuge. God's Word told me to "Be still and know that I am God" (Psalm 46:10). This has become the scripture that has taught me to trust and surrender all of me to God. Having anxiety as one of my most apparent issues, I craved stillness, but the stillness would throw me into the hands my stronghold. As I began to run to God instead, He quieted my soul as I rested in Him.

To "be still" or to "cease striving"(NASB), means to just be, to rest, to do nothing. The second half of the scripture answers the only way that you are able to be still…through knowing who God is; knowing that God is in control. How was I to trust a God whom I did not know? I was exhausted in the practicing of the eating behavior. I craved the stillness that only God could provide. When I chose to seek God first, before anything else, I began to fall in love with my God, my Creator.

> **How was I to trust a God whom I did not know?**

1. In what areas of your life do you need to "cease striving"? Do you crave the stillness that only our Lord is able to provide? Do you fear the stillness? Explain.

_____

_____

_____

2. 1 Peter 5:7 tells you to "Cast all your anxiety on Him because He cares for you." Why are you able to cast your anxiety on God?

_____

_____

_____

3. Read Psalm 103:1-8. What are God's benefits?

_____

_____

_____

_____

_____

4. How do you feel about a God that offers the above benefits? Is He one that you could trust?

_____

_____

_____

When you choose to rest in God's arms…a God who forgives, heals, redeems, and satisfies… you will feel safe. I was finally able to rest in God's arms because He was my God, the God who made me, the God who guides me, and the God who works miracles in me and through me. The God who is aware of everything about me. The God who knows "when I sit down or stand up" (Psalm 139:2, NLT), the God who knows my thoughts, the God who knows my heart, the God who wants what is best for me. The God who loves me, the God who doesn't want me to fall. The God who provides strength and comfort…the God who meets all my needs.

> **When you choose to rest in God's arms…a God who forgives, heals, redeems, and satisfies… you will feel safe.**

5. According to Isaiah 40:30-31, what benefits will you reap if you put your hope in the Lord?

___

___

___

I no longer had to fear. I finally found the hope, rest, and the strength to overcome. I had to cease striving, cease controlling my life, in order to allow God to do what He wanted to do in me, to change me, to free me.

Begin today by walking in the truth of Psalm 62:5: "Find rest, O my soul, in God alone; my hope comes from Him."

Day 3: Purge your Heart to the Lord

1. When it comes to your food stronghold, how do you feel when you are totally honest about it with:

    - yourself?

    ___

    ___

    ___

    - others?

    ___

    ___

    ___

    - God?

    ___

    ___

    ___

2. Psalm 62:8 tells us to "pour" out our hearts to God. How do you feel about "pouring" your heart out to the Lord?

_____

_____

_____

When I first began to journal my feelings, fear overcame me. What the bulimia had been hiding was trying to come out. If I wrote anything down, it meant that I had to express myself and feel. I was afraid to cry, because I thought that I would never stop. In my heart, I knew I had to begin. So…I began with "Dear Lord." At that moment I felt safe; I wasn't alone. God's presence surrounded me. I could share my heart with Him, my Creator. As I opened up my heart, the tears did come…but God was right there to meet me, to comfort me. I felt safe. I began to feel free because I had someone with whom I could share my deepest, darkest hurts, feelings, and thoughts. God's embrace…His unconditional love was immediate. That day I found my safe place in the Lord. As I was honest with God, I was able to be honest with others and myself. Every morning I looked forward to my meeting with my Lord, as I began my entry…"Dear God." God knows my heart anyway, so why not begin with Him.

Read Psalm 139:1-4 and answer the following questions.

> As I opened up my heart, the tears did come…but God was right there to meet me, to comfort me.

3. How does it make you feel that God knows your heart?

_____

_____

_____

4. Are you able to trust and share your heart with God, knowing He knows you so well?

_____

_____

_____

5. What was David's condition when he approached God in Psalm 4:1-2?

_____

_____

_____

6. What did the psalmist David do and how did God respond in Psalm 40:1-4?

_____

_____

_____

> **I was in a state of desperation when I finally cried out to the Lord.**

I was in a state of desperation when I finally cried out to the Lord. I felt ashamed to go to Him in my condition, but that is exactly how He wanted me. King Manasseh, from the Bible, is a great example of someone crying to God "as is." King Manasseh was not a follower of God. Everything he did was against God. The turning point in his life happened when he was taken as a prisoner.

Read the account in 2 Chronicles 33:1-2; 10-14, to answer the following questions.

7. How did God respond to Manasseh?

_____

_____

_____

8. Do you feel that the king deserved to be saved?

_____

_____

_____

Both David and King Manasseh came to God when "distressed." God responded to both, without questions. God wants you to come as you are. Scripture assures you that you will be heard. As you become honest with your Lord, you will be comfortable being honest with yourself and others. Believe in a God to whom you can cry out.

Day 4: Believing the Healer

God is the God of hope! God is the God who can be trusted!

1. What do you want God to do in your life?

   _____

   _____

   _____

2. Do you believe God is able to free you from your food stronghold? Explain.

   _____

   _____

   _____

Abraham, of the Old Testament, when faced with the truth that he was to become a father at the ripe age of 100, believed, when hope was against him. He didn't weaken in his faith, even "when it all seemed hopeless" (Romans 4:18, CEV). Noah built an ark, when there was no water in sight. They both did not waiver in unbelief. They were fully persuaded that God had power to do what He had promised. Their faith gave them hope.

3. In what areas do you struggle with unbelief?

   _____

   _____

   _____

4. What do you believe God is capable of doing in your life?

_____

_____

_____

> **Every time that I was filled with disbelief and wanted to give up, I pictured myself hanging from the tip of the Titanic.**

Every time that I was filled with disbelief and wanted to give up, I pictured myself hanging from the tip of the Titanic. I kept hearing God telling me, while the boat was sinking, "Don't jump ship, and hold on a little longer; safety is on the way." God hasn't and won't abandon you. He is always the same. His promises never change. It is you that changes. I recently read on a card the following, "Just when the caterpillar thought the world was over, it became a butterfly" (Author anonymous). How many times I have "jumped" ship, caved in, because I had lost all hope. How many times now, when I decide to not jump, the blessings are 100 fold. I just picture a caterpillar, looking at all the other butterflies, desiring to be one, knowing that one day it will become one, but becoming anxious while waiting, doubting it will never happen. But just when it is ready to give up, it becomes a beautiful butterfly.

Read the account of Jesus' healing of a boy in Mark 9:14-28, and answer the following questions.

5. What faith did the father have in Jesus' ability to heal in verse 22?

_____

_____

_____

6. How did Jesus respond? (vs. 23)

_____

_____

_____

7. What did the father ask of Jesus to help him with his doubt?

   _____
   _____
   _____

8. What can you do when you are faced with not trusting, hoping, and believing in the Lord's ability to heal you?

   _____
   _____
   _____

As you continue on your journey to freedom, pray without ceasing and rest in the truth that "Everything is possible to him who believes" (Mark 9:23).

Day 5: Running into the Arms of the One Who Saves

"Come to me all who are weary..." (Matthew 11:28). Running to a food stronghold, becomes wearisome.

1. What does God provide for those who come, in Matthew 11:28-30?

   _____
   _____
   _____

2. Who does Jesus invite to come?

   _____
   _____
   _____

3. What does Jesus ask you to do and what will you receive in return?

_____

_____

_____

> I believed that it was too late for me to be free from my food stronghold. It was all that I knew.

I believed that it was too late for me to be free from my food stronghold. It was all that I knew. The bulimic behavior became part of my identity. My habits were a part of me. To begin now meant that I would have to face the unfamiliar. Was it worth the effort to change now? Was it worth the pain? What other choice did I have? What was the solution?

I was weary and tired. I was waiting to be rescued. I believed food would rescue me. I waited for people to rescue me when God was the only one who had the ability.

4. Who are you hoping will rescue you besides God?

_____

_____

_____

5. What has God offered you in John 3:16-17?

_____

_____

_____

6. How do you receive this gift? (see Matthew 7:7-8)

_____

_____

_____

God offers a gift that is available to everyone who asks. Upon the acceptance of that gift, you will be given a new life. The gift is His Son, Jesus Christ, who has died for all sins (separation from God). He not only wants you...He also wants your hurts, your sins, your burdens, and your food stronghold. He just wants you to come as you are and accept the freedom and new life that is only found in Him. It is only through this relationship where you will receive total healing. It is in receiving and trusting the one whom God sent to give you a new life, His Son, not to judge, but to give life, life to the fullest.

> **God offers a gift that is available to everyone who asks**

You don't have to run anymore from what you have been suffering. When I cried out, God supplied. As I watched a seagull on the beach accepting food from a child's hand and then fly off, I realized that was exactly what it is like with God. When you come to God, or ask of Him, He is right there and grabs you. God takes you and flies off. The seagull always takes the food and flies off. Jesus stands behind the door and knocks. Are you ready to open the door and experience what He is able to do in your life? Have you ever accepted this gift of God? If you never have, make the following prayer your prayer to receive God's ultimate expression of His love.

> *Lord Jesus, I need you in my life. I ask for a new life, a life filled with your forgiveness. I claim you as my Lord and Savior, and I thank you for giving me eternal life, for loving me, and for providing the ultimate solution to my suffering. I rest in you, my safe place. I need to be saved, and I ask for the forgiveness that only comes through you.*

So come as you are into the arms of your Savior and begin this process with confidence. Trusting in the person of Jesus Christ and hoping in the Lord is the key. You don't have to run anymore from your suffering. Become "weightless" as you cast your burdens on the cross and soar above the food issues in your life.

> **So come as you are into the arms of your Savior and begin this process with confidence.**

Food for Thought

Fill in the blank with your name and repeat this truth daily.
   "I, _____, am a precious child of God." God is with me. Every day I desire to get to know my Lord and to rest in His arms and believe His Word.

Memory Verse

"Even youths grow tired and weary, and young men stumble and fall; but those who hope in the Lord will renew their strength. They will soar on wings like eagles; they will run and not grow weary, they will walk and not be faint."
Isaiah 40:30-31

Closing Prayer

Dear Lord, Thank You for sending me the gift of Your Son, Who forgives all sin. Thank You for Your grace and for loving me, despite the choices I make. Fill me with Your love as I trust You and rest in Your arms. In Jesus' name I pray.

Flying Forward

- Memorize Isaiah 40:30-31
- Start a journal. Begin each entry with "Dear God' and have a heart-to-heart with Him and see what happens!
- Read through next week's study and complete each day's questions throughout the week.

Week 3
I Like Me: Finding Your Value In God

"I praise you because I am fearfully and wonderfully made; your works are wonderful, I know that full well."
Psalm 139:14

Opening Prayer

Dear Lord, "I give thanks to You, O Lord, and I stand in awe of You, for I am wonderfully made. Marvelous are Your works! Thank You that You uniquely designed and created me, with the same care and precision You used in creating the universe…that You formed me in love exactly to Your specifications…that You embroidered me with great skill in my mother's womb" (Meyers, 56). In Jesus' name I pray.

Truth

God values me! Until you accept the truth that God sees you as perfect, you will never feel acceptable just being yourself, who God made you to be.

> God values me! Until you accept the truth that God sees you as perfect, you will never feel acceptable just being yourself, who God made you to be.

Day 1: Who are You?

I Like Me, a children's book, is about a pig that truly has a positive self-image. She truly just enjoys herself. The best part of the book is the illustrations of her body. She looks in the mirror and after saying, "Hi, good-looking!" she admires her body from her tail to her "round" tummy. Here you have an overweight pig that prances around in her underwear and is wearing a smile. How many of us can truly say, "I love my round tummy?" There is another illustration of the pig in her bathing suit, and there is that smile again. I look right at her legs, since this has always been my area of discontent. Why couldn't I have that confidence when I was in a bathing suit? How many of us are able to look in the mirror and really look at ourselves and like whom we see… no matter what?

After reading this little book, I wanted to be like this pig. I remember those days when I hid myself in big sweats and would close my eyes when I was showering, because I hated my body so much. The pain is so real. Years later, I discovered that it wasn't my body that I "hated" so much; it was me that I loathed. I know that those are strong words, but they were true. Are you able to act like this pig and wake up every morning and willingly look in the mirror and shout, "Hi beautiful"?

> I remember those days when I hid myself in big sweats and would close my eyes when I was showering, because I hated my body so much.

1. What do you say when you look at yourself in the mirror?

_____
_____
_____

God looks at you every day and loves everything about you…just because. He doesn't wait until you lose those 10 pounds or get rid of the cellulite. He doesn't wait until you find that perfect someone. He just loves you, because He created you. According to Zephaniah 3:17, "He will take great delight in you…He will rejoice over you with singing." The way the pig in *I Like Me* rejoices over herself, is the way the Lord rejoices over His children.

2. How do you feel about yourself right at this moment? What do you like or dislike?

_____
_____
_____

3. How does the truth that God "rejoices over you" affect your perception of yourself?

   _____
   _____
   _____

4. What role does your eating stronghold play in the area of your self-image (i.e., self hatred of body, form of weight control, punishing self…)?

   _____
   _____
   _____

5. When was the last time you felt good about yourself…when you felt "comfortable in your own skin"? What were the circumstances? What did you do or not do at that time?

   _____
   _____
   _____

6. In light of your answer to #5, what can you start doing or stop doing right now?

   _____
   _____
   _____

Begin today to allow God to change you from the inside out. Embrace His love for you because He made you for His enjoyment. Psalm 139:14 sums this up beautifully. We are "…fearfully and wonderfully made…" because God's "works are wonderful". The New Living Translation really brings this truth to life:

> **Begin today to allow God to change you from the inside out. Embrace His love for you because He made you for His enjoyment.**

"Thank you for making me so wonderfully complex! Your workmanship is marvelous—and how well I know it."

I am now able to see myself as God sees me, because of what He has done for me and in me. So why not rejoice over yourself knowing there is already a perfect being who rejoices over you? God desires this of you also, so what are you waiting for?

Day 2: You are God's Workmanship

1. How do you feel that God created you, and that you are not a mistake?

   _____

   _____

   _____

2. What gifts, talents, and abilities has God given you?

   _____

   _____

   _____

What I believed about myself was opposite of what God believed to be true about me. I possessed a poor self-image and had distorted vision when looking in the mirror. The God who created the heavens, the stars, and the sun…created you. The psalmist David, stands in amazement as He looks upon God's handiwork of the heavens and wonders why God would even bother with man (Psalm 8:3-4). A perfect being created you. God, who is the ultimate authority of the world created you, and He loves you no matter what you may feel about yourself.

God's Word is truth. Everything written in the Bible is true for you. I always believed what the Word said, but I never believed it was for me, because I didn't "feel" it. I thought that when I would feel it to be true, then it would be true. At the time I didn't realize that I was using food as a mask over my emotions. I didn't want to feel because I was afraid of what I would feel. I wasn't able to embrace God's truths about me, because I was so filled with my own "truths" about myself.

There was nothing positive about my truths. I was always my own critic, so if I didn't feel wonderful, beautiful, or marvelous, then that meant that I wasn't. Healing began as I replaced the "lies" which I believed about myself with God's truths…what He said about me. I needed to know what God did say about me, because what I thought about myself was destroying me.

The following chorus from the song *Your Beloved* beautifully describes what God thinks of you.

> *I am your beloved, your creation*
>
> *And you love me as I am*
>
> *You have called me, chosen for your kingdom*
>
> *Unashamed to call me your own*
>
> *I am your beloved (Helming)*

> There was nothing positive about my truths. I was always my own critic, so if I didn't feel wonderful, beautiful, or marvelous, then that meant that I wasn't.

3. According to the above chorus, who does God say you are to Him? Why does God love you?

   _____

   _____

   _____

4. Read the following scriptures and note God's truth about you and how it makes you feel.

- Psalm 139:13-14

   _____

   _____

   _____

- Isaiah 64:8

   _____

   _____

   _____

- Ephesians 2:10

___

___

___

Wow, you are God's workmanship. God is the master artist and you are His work of art.

5. How do you see yourself? And how does that affect the way you live?

___

___

___

6. How would your day be different if you lived it as a masterpiece?

___

___

___

Begin living today as a masterpiece, because that's who God says you are.

Day 3: God's Measuring Stick—Unconditional

1. When do you feel loved and accepted? (i.e. by what you do, your appearance...)

___

___

___

2. When have you experienced unconditional (complete or guaranteed, with no conditions, limitations, or provisions attached [Encarta]) love from someone? How do you receive it?

   _____

   _____

   _____

3. Do you feel loveable? Explain.

   _____

   _____

   _____

4. Whom do you admire? Why?

   _____

   _____

   _____

How was I supposed to feel better about myself and accept myself, just because God did, was a question that kept running through my mind. It wasn't until I fell in love with God and had a relationship with Him, that I could love myself...just as I was. I didn't have to be perfect, I didn't have to look perfect, and I didn't have to "feel" perfect. What mattered was that God loved me perfectly. God's love is agape love. This love "seeks to sacrificially meet the greatest need of the other, regardless of the worth, performance, or responsiveness of the other" (Moneypenny).

5. Is God's agape love for you based on how you look or perform? How does the truth that God loves you just the way you are, affect how you see yourself?

   _____

   _____

   _____

6. Read Psalm 139:1-4. What does God know about you?

_____

_____

_____

7. What would you start doing differently today knowing that God knows everything about you, your every thought (no matter what you think about yourself), and loves you?

_____

_____

_____

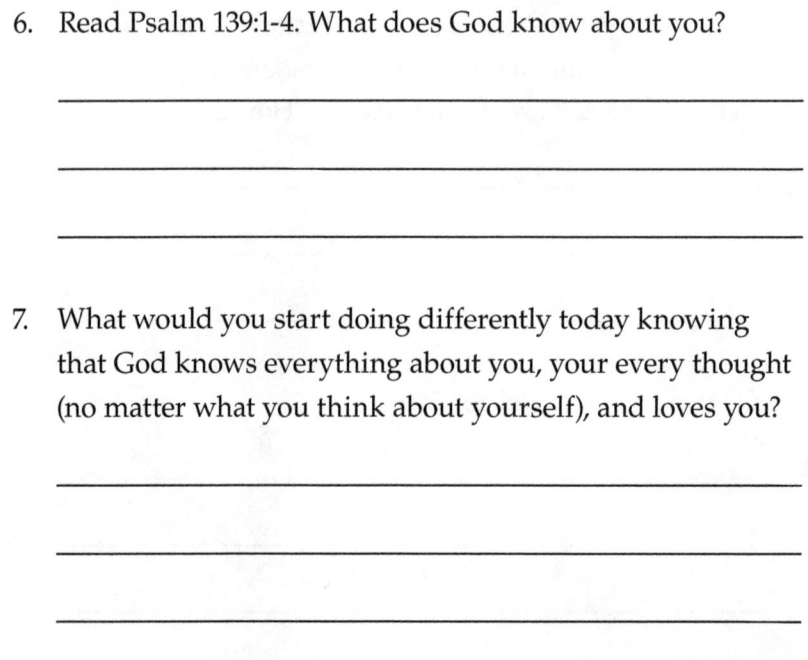

It does not matter if you "feel" love for yourself. What matters is what God thinks, what God feels about you. God is the ultimate authority and what He thinks is what matters. His Word is truth and it is meant for you.

My self-worth was based on a number or size. I could wake up in the morning feeling wonderful, and then it was time to get dressed. I would pick out my clothes and then…devastation would hit. If my pants were too tight, my day would be ruined. How could a pair of pants have so much power to ruin my whole day? I would play mind games to justify the tight pants (check the size, were they put in the dryer?), in an attempt to have a better day. My head would be filled with negative, self-destructive thoughts, beginning with, "If I am fat anyway, then I will just eat more." I took this to mean that I was not perfect. I would then punish myself by running to food and eventually purging.

> **My self-worth was based on a number or size.**

What was really going on? I just didn't want to feel, not only the emotions but also my skin against the fabric. The pants were suffocating. I would want to die. This made me realize how much power I would give a number. How could I wake up one minute happy (wearing "baggy" pajamas) and then the next minute become miserable because my pants were tight. This was when I realized that there was more to the bulimia and food issues, then just being a "weight" thing. I realized the real power was in the number. It would be the same with a scale. Great day if clothes fit or if the number on the scale was low…but if too high or tight clothes, miserable day. How superficial. I was allowing a pant size to dictate my day. I truly believed that I would be happy only when I reached a certain size and weight…but would any size or weight be enough? The funny thing is that people see me as me, not as a size or weight, so why couldn't I?

8. Close your eyes. Picture yourself standing across from yourself. Answer the following:

- How would you describe yourself?
  _____
  _____
  _____

- How would someone else describe you?
  _____
  _____
  _____

- Now put on "God's Glasses", believing what He says about you. How would God describe you?
  _____
  _____
  _____

- In what ways can God's words affect your future choices and behaviors?
  _____
  _____
  _____

When you base your joy/happiness on your appearance—your body, your clothes, your weight—you will always be disappointed. Your looks change. Every day you are a day older. Your

> **When you base your joy/happiness on your appearance—your body, your clothes, your weight—you will always be disappointed.**

weight fluctuates. If you use your size as a barometer for your feelings, then you will base your feelings on what the number is. People may compliment you, but that is temporary. One day you may not even get one compliment. Does that then mean you are ugly, fat, gross, and unacceptable? You can never measure up. You will never be pretty enough, thin enough, young enough. There will always be someone who is prettier, smaller, taller, or thinner. You will never feel enough or be enough because you are constantly measuring who you are by your externals.

When your self-worth is based on who you are in Christ, you can be joyful no matter what. God never changes. He doesn't change His mind about how He feels about you. It is what God thinks that really matters. Right now where you are, despite your weight or how you feel…God loves you. God finds you acceptable. As you accept this truth on the inside it will shine on the outside.

Day 4: Satan's Playing Field— You Can Have It All

1. What are some of the messages that society and the media tell you about appearance and self-image? Which messages do you desire?

   _____

   _____

   _____

> **My life's goal was to be thin.**

My life's goal was to be thin. I didn't think that there was anything wrong with that, because "everyone" was consumed with appearance and trying to acquire the perfect body. It was attainable…the media said so. There was a diet and exercise plan that could fit anyone's lifestyle. If you didn't like the color of your hair, you could change the color; if your nose was too big, have plastic surgery; if you wanted a model's body, starve yourself. The sky was the limit. Life was about never being quite content about your body because you could always look better. Critical thinking…tearing yourself apart so you could then rebuild yourself into what you want to be. I bought into the magazines and all the quick solutions to weight loss. No wonder I never felt that I was enough, because I could be better.

It wasn't a burden to diet and exercise; it was just a way of life. I didn't stand out because everyone was doing it. Well, I bought into the many lies of the world. I could attain the so-called "perfect," if I worked really hard. What kind of life was that? There had to be more. What I didn't realize was that I was being deceived.

2. Read 1 Samuel 16:7. What does man look at? What does God see when He looks at you?

   _____
   _____
   _____

3. In light of the above scripture, and what you know about God, how does it make you feel that God's opinion of you is not dependent on a pant size or a number on the scale?

   _____
   _____
   _____

4. What words describe satan and his role, from the following scriptures?

   - John 8:44

     _____
     _____
     _____

   - Revelation 12:9

     _____
     _____
     _____

- Revelation 12:10

_____

_____

_____

Satan steers us from the truth. He leads the world astray. He is the accuser, the father of lies. He wants you to believe that there is an easier way to freedom, but it in turn puts us in bondage. Your health is a priority, but looking good has been the world's focus. We jeopardize our health to look good. Diets and quick fixes are more acceptable than Christ. People just swarm the bookstores, like I did, to buy the newest book with the perfect solution to weight loss. We read the book, try it. We become in bondage to the thing that was supposed to bring freedom.

Satan wants you to buy into the lies of the world, that you can have it all and look perfect. Satan knows God is the answer. Satan knows that he has been defeated. Satan's only triumph comes when God's children are in bondage. I find that when I share that I have freedom through Christ, some listen, but then someone else will bring up the perfect diet and everyone is excited and wants to try it. Satan steers you from the truth that the Lord is the answer. Satan's accusations do not have any power when you choose not to agree with them.

There is no such thing as quick fixes. They are exactly what that term is…quick. You may get a quick result, but it is only temporary. If there was such a thing as the perfect diet, why are so many new ones coming up?

> **Satan wants you to buy into the lies of the world, that you can have it all and look perfect.**

5. What quick fixes have you bought into? Have any of them worked?

_____

_____

_____

6. List what you feel you have "to be" (i.e. smaller/larger pant size, lower/higher weight…) before you can accept yourself as God accepts you? Then go through the list and write truth or lie next to them.

_____
_____
_____

7. Do you truly believe that you would accept yourself if your "list" was to come true?

_____
_____
_____

Satan's lies: You can be perfect; you can only be loved if you behave and look perfectly. God doesn't demand perfection because God is perfection. He wants you. Stop believing the lies and measuring yourself by the world's measuring stick. Only one person is perfect, and that is Jesus. When we accept Christ's sacrifice on the cross, He covers us, so God sees us as perfect; You have achieved it, through Christ.

Day 5: God's Plan

1. Do you believe that there is something that you could do that would change God's attitude toward you?

_____
_____
_____

2. What do you think God is thinking of you when you are running to a food stronghold?

_____

_____

_____

3. How does the statement that "God loves you no matter what" change your opinion of yourself? What would you do differently?

_____

_____

_____

> **Satan has come to steal what the Lord has given you. Jesus has come to give you life abundantly (John 10:10).**

Satan has come to steal what the Lord has given you. Jesus has come to give you life abundantly (John 10:10). Satan is the problem, and God has provided the solution. The trial of your food stronghold that you are experiencing now is stealing from you the life that you deserve in Christ. Don't let satan steal from you anymore. Jesus has conquered satan and provides you the peace and joy that you deserve, the peace and the joy that satan tries to steal from you every day. You can have all that…in Jesus Christ.

Cherry Boone, who suffered with anorexia and bulimia, believed that healing came when she started to believe that she was lovable, even in her food strongholds. Even with her failures and her sins, she was still valued and cared for unconditionally by her God (Boone, 158). God's love for you is not dependent on your behavior. Your peace and joy may be affected, but His love for you is untouched.

4. Read Romans 5:6-8 and answer the following.

- How did God demonstrate His love for you?

_____

_____

_____

- According to the above scripture, what was our condition when God sacrificed His Son for us?

  _____
  _____
  _____

- What does that tell you about God's love?

  _____
  _____
  _____

5. According to John 3:17, Jesus came to save the world, not to condemn. Do you condemn yourself? If so, in what ways?

   _____
   _____
   _____

God lavished His love on us "while we were still sinners", and as Ephesians 2:5 describes, the time of Christ's sacrifice was "…even when we were dead in transgressions…". If He was willing to sacrifice His own Son, why wouldn't He accept you or me right now?

6. According to Psalm 32:1-2, how does God handle your sin?

   _____
   _____
   _____

7. What is your role in the forgiveness of sins? (1 John 1:9)

   _____
   _____
   _____

8. Have you ever forgiven yourself for having a food stronghold in your life or for not being able to perform perfectly? Explain.

_____

_____

_____

> **Not only did God prove His love to us by sacrificing His Son, He also provided the forgiveness of sins and eternal life.**

Not only did God prove His love to us by sacrificing His Son, He also provided the forgiveness of sins and eternal life. God doesn't count your sins against you (Psalm 32:1-2). It is too amazing to fathom. His grace is undeserved, "infinite love, mercy, favor, and goodwill shown to humankind" (Encarta). God's love is amazing. God is faithful to forgive all of your sins. The joy of the Lord comes from the truth that He forgives you and loves you, just because…no questions asked. Living in this truth is the strength needed to overcome.

Daily make this truth your own.

I, _____, am filled with joy because the Lord loves me and offers total forgiveness and salvation in His Son.

True freedom is not being obsessed about anything but God…being able to be all you can be through Christ and finding your value in Christ. Don't allow a size or number on the scale to define you. There is freedom in taking the proper care of your body and accepting yourself right now…. whether or not your body is acceptable to you right now. This body is a temporal shell, just like the home where you live today, whether it is an apartment or a mansion. God wants you to care for both in the proper fashion, but it is more about what is on the inside, which will last forever.

Food for Thought

WHEN I SAY, "I AM A CHRISTIAN"

When I say, "I am a Christian"
I'm not shouting, "I've been saved!"
I'm whispering, "I get lost!
That's why I chose this way"

When I say, "I am a Christian"
I don't speak with human pride
I'm confessing that I stumble—
Needing God to be my guide

When I say, "I am a Christian"
I'm not trying to be strong
I'm professing that I'm weak
And pray for strength to carry on

When I say, "I am a Christian"
I'm not bragging of success
I'm admitting that I've failed
And cannot ever pay the debt

When I say, "I am a Christian"
I don't think I know it all
I submit to my confusion
Asking humbly to be taught

When I say, "I am a Christian"
I'm not claiming to be perfect
My flaws are all too visible
But God believes I'm worth it

When I say, "I am a Christian"
I still feel the sting of pain
I have my share of heartache,
Which is why I seek His name

When I say, "I am a Christian"
I do not wish to judge
I have no authority...
I only know I'm loved

Used by Permission
Copyright 1988 Carol Wimmer

Memory Verse

"I praise you because I am fearfully and wonderfully made; your works are wonderful, I know that full well."
Psalm 139:14

Closing Prayer

Dear Lord, Thank You for creating me just the way You wanted, everything about me, even my flaws and temperament. You formed me according to Your plans, as Your plans are perfect. Thank You that You love me unconditionally. Help me to accept Your love, even when I feel unlovely. Help me to find my value in You. In Jesus' name I pray.

Flying Forward

- Memorize Psalm 139:14
- Read through next week's study and complete each day's questions throughout the week.

Week 4

God Is My Stronghold

*"The LORD is my rock, my fortress and my deliverer;
my God is my rock, in whom I take refuge, my shield
and the horn of my salvation, my stronghold."*
Psalm 18:2

Opening Prayer

Dear Lord, I open my heart to You. I am choosing You to be my stronghold, my rock, and my refuge. Fill me with Your Holy Spirit as I begin to let go of my food stronghold. In Jesus' name I pray.

Truth

God is my stronghold.

Food for Thought

<u>Goodbye Old Friend</u>
When I was sad, I would run to you
When I was lonely, you were there to bring comfort
When I was frustrated, I could take it all out on you
When I was angry, I could punish myself with you
You were the lord of my life
You were always there and I could use you for whatever role I
　wanted you to play
First bringing comfort, then pain
You began to destroy me, yet I couldn't let you go
I didn't want you anymore, but who else did I have
Where would I go if I needed comfort, to hide, to protect myself
Who could do what I allowed you to do
I thought you could save me…I gave you way too much power
It is time to say goodbye
I found your replacement
I found a place where I can go when my needs aren't met by others

> God is my stronghold.

> I found a place where I can go and be myself, and not be judged
> I found a place where I can run and be safe
> I found a place where I am always accepted
> I found a place where I can feel all of my emotions
> I found a place where I no longer fear
> I found a place where I am truly saved
> I found a place
> My Father's arms
> So goodbye, my old friend, you are no longer needed in my life
> You have to go, because there is no room for other idols in my Father's arms
> He is all I need
> He is my fortress, my refuge, my stronghold
> He is my Lord

Day 1: Is Food a Stronghold for You?

1. Are you at rest or restless when you are running to or away from food?

   _____
   _____
   _____

2. What does your eating behavior provide for you?

   _____
   _____
   _____

3. Reflect on Psalm 62:5-7. What does God provide?

   _____
   _____
   _____

A stronghold is a false form of protection, a concrete fortress you have constructed around your life. It is something that you don't need to survive, but believe you need to survive. A stronghold is a coping mechanism.

In the Bible, the Israelites would hide in strongholds. Strongholds were fortresses with difficult access, a place of protection. Food was my hiding place, my place of protection. When the food wasn't enough, I could run to the bigger fortress of bulimia. What started as a safe place for me, grew into a prison, a place of bondage. I was in bondage to food; whether restricting or binging. Anabel Gillham, of Lifetime Guarantee Ministries, sums up the meaning of a stronghold perfectly: "Destructive patterns in your life that have become so deeply entrenched that you perform them habitually, not even recognizing that you are exhibiting 'unchrist-like' behavior or that you have a choice in resisting them" (Gillham, 6).

> A stronghold is a false form of protection, a concrete fortress you have constructed around your life. It is something that you don't need to survive, but believe you need to survive. A stronghold is a coping mechanism.

4. Would you describe your relationship to food as a stronghold? If yes, in what ways does it "hold you" or take control of you?

_____

_____

_____

> Food was my hiding place, my place of protection.

5. How would you describe a food stronghold?

_____

_____

_____

I thought I had a hold on food, when instead food had a hold on me, a strong hold. I would dream about the day that I would be free of the bulimia. That day of freedom meant that Jesus would take away the bulimia and give me a perfect body. I would have it all. I actually wanted freedom for all the wrong reasons. I was more focused on just getting rid of the behavior without changing my nature. I wanted God to reach His hand down and just stop my behavior in the middle of it. I kept in my stronghold and was waiting. God doesn't work like that. I was bowing down to my stronghold and not to my God. There is no room for "idols" in God's kingdom. He wasn't going to just whisk away something that I was honoring. I just wanted the behavior changed and I didn't want to have to do anything. Why should I? I was the one suffering wasn't I? I didn't put this on myself, it was because of others. Didn't I deserve to be free of this? Okay God prove yourself to me and take this away? Just as I thought I found how to "have my cake and eat it too", I also thought I found my own theology…I can just keep sinning, worshipping my idol while waiting for God to heal me. I had a lot to learn.

Wow, what a bunch of lies that were in my head. Who really was God? The God I was depending on was not the God of the Bible. I was a rebellious child full of pride. In the movie *Finding Nemo*, the fish Dory chants, "Just keep swimming, swimming, swimming, just keep swimming…". Well, I kept swimming in food strongholds. I would have been better off just being eaten by a shark.

> **Wow, what a bunch of lies that were in my head.**

6. *He (Jesus) didn't come to change our behavior; He came to change our nature (Anderson, et.al.).* What do you want Jesus to do with the food stronghold in your life?

_____

_____

_____

7. Are you waiting to be rescued from your stronghold?

_____

_____

_____

8. *"Indulging our fleshly appetites does not satisfy them; indulgence only creates a greater dependency upon those things we crave. Only those who hunger and thirst for righteousness will be satisfied"* (Anderson, et.al., 41).

   - How does the first part of this statement describe the practice of the food stronghold in your life?

     _____
     _____
     _____

   - Who are the ones who will be satisfied? Do you have a hunger for God?

     _____
     _____
     _____

Begin today to feed yourself with God, because, as Matthew 5:6 says,

"You're blessed when you've worked up a good appetite for God. He's food and drink in the best meal you'll ever eat." (MSG).

Day 2: Letting Go

1. Picture yourself without your food stronghold. What thoughts and emotions come to mind?

   _____
   _____
   _____

2. How do you feel knowing that you can be free?

   _____
   _____
   _____

> Giving up the bulimia, and the control I had over food, was like giving up an old friend.

Giving up the bulimia, and the control I had over food, was like giving up an old friend. Complete freedom from the food stronghold in my life happened when I totally surrendered them to the Lord. I had surrendered myself to God, yet was still holding onto the bulimia and the behaviors that went with it. The Lord wanted all of me, not just a part. In order for me to be totally free, He had to have all of me. I remember the day I was crying out to the Lord for Him to just take the binging and purging away. I imagined a little crying Joni, all curled up in a ball, inside my stomach. I felt that if I were to give up the bulimic behavior, I would be giving up myself, this hurting Joni. I didn't want to let her go because I believed that giving up the stronghold meant I was giving up myself. I was like two people in one. The food stronghold became who I was. Who would I be without it? It was my identity. The little girl inside of me hurt so much. She was the only Joni I knew. I was protecting her with the bulimia. I feared that if I truly was to give it up to the Lord, He would take it away and then what would be left.

> Embracing the truths that God loved me and was with me always, removed the fear.

I was a new creation in Christ when I committed my life to Him, and that was where my identity could be found. Embracing the truths that God loved me and was with me always, removed the fear. It was at that point that I gave the bulimia and the little crying Joni to God, and allowed Him to fill the void that was left. He was right there. He became my comfort, my stronghold. It was at that point that I totally surrendered myself to the Lord, which began the process of becoming the Joni that He made me to be.

3. Have you totally surrendered your control over food to the Lord? If not, what do you believe is holding you back?

___

___

___

4. Reflect on the following scriptures. Note how this is true of your food stronghold when it is the Lord of your life, and what is true of God when He is your Stronghold.

- Psalm 31:2-3

  _____
  _____
  _____

- Psalm 27:1-2

  _____
  _____
  _____

- Psalm 62:6

  _____
  _____
  _____

- Psalm 18:30-33

  _____
  _____
  _____

5. Do you truly believe God is enough to take the place of your stronghold? Why or why not?

   _____
   _____
   _____

> **God provides everything for you because He is everything.**

God provides everything for you because He is everything. God lights the path you should follow in order to overcome any stronghold in your life. Make God your strength, your rock, your refuge, your stronghold, and in Him you will not be shaken.

"If you want Him to take your burden, He must have all of you, not simply the problem you want removed. As you allow Christ to control you, He will, in fact, be dealing with your burden" (Stanley, *"How to…"*).

Day 3: Trading Ownership

Destruction of the Fortress

A food stronghold is also an idol. An idol can be defined as a false god. I didn't realize that I was "worshipping" the eating behaviors I practiced. I was bowing down to the food. I gave it power that it really didn't have.

1. According to Colossians 3:5, what are you to do with idols in your life?

   _____

   _____

   _____

I tried it all. I tried every diet, every "self-help" book, therapy, and a nutritionist. All of these are wonderful tools, but when used without Christ, they are worthless. I would always just get so close, but never fully succeed in the abolishment of the stronghold. My focus was still on the behavior. I knew I needed something more. To rid myself of this stronghold, which was strangling the life out of me, I needed the power of God. Eating behaviors became idols in my life because that was where my focus was.

> I tried it all. I tried every diet, every "self-help" book, therapy, and a nutritionist.

2. How would you describe a food stronghold as an idol?

   _____

   _____

   _____

Every morning, when I would wake up, fear about starting a new day would overtake me. Thoughts of, "will I binge/purge today, what will trigger me, what do I need to protect myself from, will my clothes fit, how will I get everything done...", would overtake my mind. I would wake up defeated. These questions would then lead me into negative thinking patterns, believing lies about who I was. The only choice that was left for me was to take the hand of my good old buddy bulimia and we would travel through the day. The food was my hiding place, my fortress to protect me. It was "my" food stronghold, and I was the owner. It gave me something that I knew I could control that day. Since I couldn't control my thoughts, I could control the food. I had my bulimia to stop them.

Ownership allowed me to use it as I wished, whenever I wanted to, and it would always be there for me…unless I chose to sell it. Being an owner of a business is all consuming and tiring. Like a workaholic, it was robbing my days of my joy. The day I finally decided to sell my stronghold was the day my freedom began. I was no longer the owner. I got rid of my rights, my control. Instead, I placed myself under new ownership. I was God's. I traded it in for God.

The following lyrics from the song "Trading My Sorrows" describe my experience. When you give up something, you need to fill that spot. It is what we replace it with that will determine our well being. I chose God. The bulimia was my sorrow, my shame, my sickness, and my pain. Now... "His joy came in my mornings".

I'm trading my sorrows. I'm trading my shame. I'm laying them down for the joy of the Lord. I'm trading my sickness. I'm trading my pain. I'm laying them down for the joy of the Lord. I'm pressed, but not crushed; persecuted, not abandoned; struck down, but not destroyed. I am blessed beyond the curse, for His promise will endure that His joy is going to be my strength. Though my sorrows may last for the night His joy comes with the morning (Evans).

3. How does it feel "owning" your stronghold? Is it something you want to sell?

_____
_____
_____

4. When you sell your stronghold, who will you give it to? Do you want to trade it in for God?

   _____

   _____

   _____

5. Read 2 Corinthians 4:8-9. After you have practiced the eating behavior, do you feel "crushed, despair, abandoned, and destroyed?" What does the Word say when you are feeling hard pressed, perplexed, and persecuted, and you trade your stronghold in for Christ?

   _____

   _____

   _____

6. Ask God to show you what else you need to trade in for Christ.

   _____

   _____

   _____

With God on your side, "...*Everything is possible for him who believes*" (Mark 9:23).

Day 4: Bringing the Lies to the Surface

> **Strongholds come from false ideas, and false ideas come from satan.**

Strongholds come from false ideas, and false ideas come from satan. They are frauds, worthless, and have no power in them, only the power you may give them. Lies fill your head convincing you that you "need" your food stronghold in order to survive. It is all you have. You believe it is working because you are surviving, but barely.

1. Read Isaiah 44:20. What misleads you into the behavior?

   _____

   _____

   _____

2. Do you believe that a food stronghold is a lie? Why?

   _____

   _____

   _____

The main lies about a food stronghold are that you need it to survive and that food is the enemy. Satan led me astray. Satan deceived me. It was all a lie. A food stronghold masquerades as a solution to a problem. What is it hiding? As long as you run to the stronghold, you will never get to the reasons behind it. Satan wants you to be brokenhearted and desperate, therefore running to take cover, finding alternative solutions. He wants you to believe that there is hope in it. As long as I was spending my time controlling food, by restricting or binging, then I wouldn't have to get behind the behavior to see what was really going on. I took a good thing, food that is needed to nourish the body, and turned it into a bad thing. Food can't deliver...God can.

> The main lies about a food stronghold are that you need it to survive and that food is the enemy. satan led me astray.

3. If the stronghold that you are practicing could talk, what would it say to you? Have a conversation with it. What would you say to it? Note any emotions, perspectives, which come up.

   _____

   _____

   _____

4. What does your stronghold promise you? (i.e., I will take away your pain, I will love you). Refer back to your answers on question 1 for help.

_____

_____

_____

> A food stronghold is more than a bondage to the abuse of food. It is a bondage to many different emotions.

A food stronghold is more than a bondage to the abuse of food. It is a bondage to many different emotions. Anorexia, bulimia, and compulsive overeating are symptoms, a reaction, to an underlying cause. It isn't about stopping or controlling the behavior; it is about healing what is causing the behavior. A food stronghold is covering a wounded heart that Jesus wants to heal. The behavior may be the last thing to go, but when the root is taken care of, true freedom is found.

The Food Diary

An effective tool that helps to get to the underlying reasons behind the food behavior is a food diary. It helps you to get to the underlying emotions that trigger you into the behavior. These emotions are the doorway into your hurts that are fueling the behavior. It gets to the heart and that is where healing begins. So...what is really behind your refrigerator door?

When you are reaching for or denying yourself the food, the food takes on a whole different meaning. What is really going on when you reach for the ice cream? It is no longer ice cream. It is not vanilla, chocolate, or strawberry. It may become loneliness, or bitterness, or anger, or any emotion. If you restrict your intake of food, the food you are denying yourself also takes on a new meaning. What is the stronghold protecting? What is fueling the behavior?

Begin today filling out the food diary (as shown in sample). A blank food diary is provided in Appendix A, at the back of the book. Please make copies and continue to fill out for at least two weeks. Remember, it is not about the food. This tool is for you and does not have to be shared. You will be recording the time, behavior (binging, purging, starving...), emotions, circumstances, and food involved when you run to the stronghold. The next time you reach for food or deny yourself, what are you really looking for? Ask yourself, when you are about to binge or restrict your food, what emotional label is that food wearing. Give the food the new name.

A sample diary is filled out below. Sometimes you may not even know what you are feeling, just record what you can.

Food Diary

Time	Behavior	Circumstance/Event	Emotions/mood "I feel/I am"	Food Eaten or denied
8:00am	Binge	Breakfast/ no one is home	I am lonely	Fruit, cereal, toast, cookies, doughnut...
8:15	Exercise	Clothes don't fit	I feel fat	Nothing
11:00	Binge/purge	Phone call with friend	I feel rejected	Leftovers, desserts
5:00 pm	Binge	Have nothing to wear	I feel frustrated	Everything
6:00	Starve	Party	I don't deserve to eat	Nothing
10:00	Binge	Home	No one loves me	Ice cream, potato chips, cheese, spaghetti...

Day 5: No Need to Hide

1. Where is God when you are turning to a food stronghold for comfort? (Psalm 139:7-12)

   _____

   _____

   _____

2. How do you feel about running to God? Do you ever feel like hiding from God? Why or why not?

_____

_____

_____

After Adam and Eve sinned in the garden, they "tried" hiding from God because of their shame (Genesis 3:9-10). Instead of running to God for help, they ran away. Shame is an emotion of feeling unworthy, undeserving.

3. Have you ever felt shame? If yes, explain when.

_____

_____

_____

You can't hide from God in anything or anywhere. He is everywhere, as He is omnipresent. Hiding in a food stronghold is temporary. God is there waiting for you to run to Him. I felt as if my only option was to run to my food stronghold. God was right there, watching me, holding His hand out, always available, but I wouldn't take it. Instead I took the hand of the food, something tangible, and something I could hold onto.

God was always there, but I wasn't looking. Why would He want me, especially the way that I was feeling? One day, as I was sitting at the beach, I watched a father and a young child. The child was happy, laughing and playing in the sand. It came time to leave and the father called his son. The child would not go. The child just sat there kicking his feet and screaming. The father continued to walk away, yet keeping an eye on his son. The child finally got up, ran to the father and the father immediately scooped him up in his hands, and accepted him as they walked away together. The father accepted the child in his rebellion. He was there for him.

In the midst of my eating behavior, in my rebellion, in my

> **God was always there, but I wasn't looking.**

feelings of unworthiness, God was always there just waiting to swoop me up in His arms, but I had to choose to run to Him. When I finally did run to Him, He took me, and nothing has been the same since.

4. How do you feel knowing that God is omnipresent?

   _____
   _____
   _____

5. Why would God's omnipresence and unconditional love for you provide a safe place for you to run?

   _____
   _____
   _____

6. Read Psalm 32:1-7 and answer the following.

   - What happened when the psalmist kept silent? (vs.3)

     _____
     _____
     _____

   - What action did he take in verse 5, and how did God respond?

     _____
     _____
     _____

   - What did God become to the writer in verse 7?

     _____
     _____
     _____

Food for Thought

"God always wills for you to be free from strongholds. We may not always be sure God wills to heal us of every disease or prosper us with tangible blessings. But He always 'wills' to free us from strongholds" (Moore, 32-33).

Memory Verse

"The LORD is my rock, my fortress and my deliverer; my God is my rock, in whom I take refuge, my shield and the horn of my salvation, my stronghold."
Psalm 18:2

Closing Prayer

Dear Lord, Thank You that You are always available to me, no matter how I may be feeling or acting, and that You are a safe place. Thank You for your strength as I begin to uncover emotions that I have stuffed. It brings me great comfort knowing that You are right here with me through this process. In Jesus' name I pray.

Flying Forward

- Memorize 2 Samuel 22:3

- Minimize your eating stronghold throughout your recovery. It is not who you are. You can live with joy, right now, even though you may still be struggling with the behavior. Picture putting the food stronghold in a little box so that it becomes something that can be dealt with.

- Throughout the week do the following exercise: How do you feel, what emotions emerge, when you read the following statements concerning your stronghold to food or to other strongholds you have in your life…
    - My stronghold to _____ is not who I am (minimize it).
    - My stronghold to _____ can be demolished.

- I can survive without my stronghold to
  _____.

- Christ is able to set me free from my stronghold to
  _____.

- I deserve to be free from my stronghold to
  _____.

- Read through next week's study and complete each day's questions throughout the week.

Week 5
Putting A Face On The Food Stronghold

"He heals the brokenhearted and binds up their wounds."
Psalm 147:3

"Therefore, there is now no condemnation for those who are in Christ Jesus."
Romans 8:1

Opening Prayer

Dear Lord, I come before You as You begin to uncover the reasons that are behind the food stronghold. Give me wisdom to know why I have chosen food as my stronghold. Comfort me and protect me and let Your presence be known. In Jesus' name I pray.

Truth

God heals my broken heart and restores me.

> God heals my broken heart and restores me.

Day 1: Why Food?

Do you ever wonder why it is that food has become a stronghold in your life? I always wondered why I ran to food and not another coping mechanism. In my journal time, God brought me back to the first time I used food in an unhealthy manner. It was at this time, I believe, the bulimic behavior was birthed.

Why does food have so much control? Why is food the drug of choice? Basically, food is very accessible. We have to eat to survive. It is acceptable to eat food. It is okay to talk about food. Food tastes good. Food seems so innocent, yet it has the potential to cause pain. When does it become so dangerous?

> Do you ever wonder why it is that food has become a stronghold in your life?

Putting A Face On The Food Stronghold / 67

Take one cookie. A cookie is a little circle of sugar that entices you. When does this cookie become a monster? A cookie is innocent. A cookie tastes so good. A cookie is a treat. Yes, one cookie, or two cookies is a treat. What happens when that one cookie becomes a dozen? What happens when the cookie becomes the forbidden fruit? What happens when the cookie has more control than you have? It quickly loses its innocence. What started as something so small gives birth to a monster. A monster is defined as "a threatening force" (Merriam-Webster). A monster is an enemy. Food has become your friend, yet your worst enemy.

Food became the comfort, the friend, when nothing or no one else was there. I had a love/hate relationship with food. Food served a different purpose in my life than providing nutrition. Food started as something fun. It would bring people together at social gatherings—until it became the honored guest. It just taste so good that I couldn't walk away. The "tastes" would linger in my mouth. I would have to have more.

> **Food became the comfort, the friend, when nothing or no one else was there. I had a love/hate relationship with food.**

Little did I know that the food was just a mask, just a covering, and a Band Aid over my emotions and pain. What was I really craving? I was so unhappy inside that anything that brought me any pleasure, I would gobble it up.

I started my first diet in 5th grade at the age of 11. The triggering event was when I overheard a negative comment about my body from a family friend. I interpreted that to mean that I wasn't perfect. How could I regain the perfection that I thought I had achieved through all my performances? Up to that point in my life, I was always performing in order to be the perfect child. Whatever I could make perfect I would. This incident triggered me. I believe this was the birth, first stage, of my "Cookie Monster."

1. What "role" did food play in your family of origin? Look at your childhood relationship to food. How was it used or controlled in your family? How did you see food?

_____

_____

_____

2. What is your earliest memory of using food in an unhealthy manner? How old were you, who was there, what were the circumstances (i.e., first diet, first binge, first starving episode…), the emotions felt?

_____

_____

_____

3. What purpose did the food serve at the time of your earliest memory?

_____

_____

_____

Day 2: God's Face

As explained in the previous chapter, a stronghold is a hiding place. This hiding place is serving a purpose in your life. What has proven instrumental in my recovery has been "putting a face" on the unhealthy eating behaviors I practiced. *Who or what did the food stronghold represent?* I often wondered if the bulimia had a face, who/what would it be? It has a face or faces. A food stronghold is false and is a covering. It is masking something. My prayer for you is to find the face that your stronghold is wearing (this face will be revealed throughout the recovery process).

> My prayer for you is to find the face that your stronghold is wearing…

1. What do you think you are seeking when you turn to or away from food?

_____

_____

_____

2. What does Psalm 105:4 tell you to do?

   _____
   _____
   _____

3. What does "seeking" God's face mean to you?

   _____
   _____
   _____

   A special friend of mine sent me a card with the words, "I miss your face." It spoke volumes to me. I use that expression all the time with my children when I am thinking about them and they are not with me. What I really miss is all of them, everything about them. Their faces tell it all. Their faces make me smile. It is the same with God…His face. When I seek God's face, I am seeking Him, everything that He is. I crave His presence and a relationship with Him. I smile as I think about who He is and what He has done for me and continues to do…when I choose to seek Him.

   > A special friend of mine sent me a card with the words, "I miss your face."

4. Refer to Numbers 6:24-26. What happens when you experience God's face upon you?

   _____
   _____
   _____

5. Where does seeking a stronghold lead you? (Proverbs 14:12; Matthew 7:13)

   _____
   _____
   _____

6. How would you describe the face of a food stronghold?

   _____
   _____
   _____

7. What are some of the characteristics of the face of a food stronghold in your life that you are beginning to see?

   _____
   _____
   _____

Day 3: Trust the Controller

The bulimic years—the bulimia was a veil that covered my true self. This food stronghold shielded me from the world. It was my protection. It was all mine. No one could take it away. I had total control over it and my life…so I thought. I used the overeating and bulimia when I wanted to. It was my secret. I could enjoy all the foods I wanted and then purge them out. It served a purpose in my life. What was it really covering? What were the bulimic behavior and the obsession of being thin really masking? Why did I feel that I needed this for survival?

Instead of facing my hurts and wounds, and labeling them as hurts and wounds, I starved them, fed them, and purged them. Look back to your earliest memory of using food in an unhealthy manner, from Day One. Ask God to reveal to you what you were trying to accomplish in the stronghold. Answer the question(s) below, which pertain to you (it is okay if you don't know at this time).

> **Instead of facing my hurts and wounds, and labeling them as hurts and wounds, I starved them, fed them, and purged them.**

1. What were you really "starving" when you ran away from food?

   _____

   _____

   _____

2. What were you really "feeding" when you ran to food?

   _____

   _____

   _____

3. What were you really "purging" when you purged the food?

   _____

   _____

   _____

All food issues consist of some form of control over food. When an area of your life is out of control, you cling to something that you are able to control, such as your body and food. Meanwhile, you are so focused on the management of the behavior (i.e., controlling it) that you are really out of control.

4. What do you believe you have control over in your life?

   _____

   _____

   _____

5. What and/or who do you try to control?

   _____

   _____

   _____

6. What do you think you are controlling with a food stronghold?

_____

_____

_____

7. What do Ecclesiastes 7:13-14, Psalm 115:3, and Job 42:2 tell you about God? What does that mean to you?

_____

_____

_____

Scripture states that God is in control…of everything. If God is in control, why are our lives so out of control? In the controlling of your food intake you may be trying to control pain from the past.

8. "People who have been hurt tend to react out of their wounded emotions, rather than to act according to wisdom and the Word of God" (Meyer, 36). Does this sound true of you?

_____

_____

_____

> **The basic facts:** Pain will be pain. Hurts will be hurts. Rejection will be rejection. Circumstances will be circumstances. And God will always be God.

The basic facts: Pain will be pain. Hurts will be hurts. Rejection will be rejection. Circumstances will be circumstances. And God will always be God. The question is, What will you do with…your pain; your hurts; your wounds; your rejection; your _____; and your God?

I tried starving, binging, purging, all of the above—which backfired and caused more pain, more hurt, more wounds. Don't allow your past circumstances, past hurts, to define who you are or infect your present and future. You need to unleash these and the control to the ultimate controller…God. I made the choice to give it all to God. Are you ready to give up your control to God's control? Are you ready to give up the controlling of those things which have caused or are causing you pain, by a food stronghold, and make the choice to give up control and trust God?

Begin today to follow what Proverbs 3:4-6 says, *"Trust in the Lord with all your heart and lean not on your own understanding; in all your ways acknowledge Him, and He will make your paths straight"*, and you will be giving control back to the only one who has the real control.

Day 4: Deserved to be Punished

Damaged freight

I was destroyed. I was in the rubble. My pain demolished me. I felt crucified. I was wounded, wounded badly. I lived from the position of damaged, destroyed. The only thing I knew was destruction. I punished myself for feeling, for not being enough, for mistakes, for being me. It was the only thing that I knew.

1. How have you felt the devastation as described above? Explain.

   _____

   _____

   _____

The abuse of food in your life is a form of punishment, an abuse of yourself. Where did you hear the lie that you deserved to be punished? In the book *The Monster Within*, the author who struggled with bulimia and anorexia, had a major breakthrough in her recovery process when she was able to answer the question of, "When did you become damaged freight?" The feeling of being damaged freight is birthed by past hurts or wounds (emotional injury [Encarta]) in your life.

> **The abuse of food in your life is a form of punishment, an abuse of yourself.**

You carry around those wounds and respond from a position of damage and unworthiness, which leads to destructive behaviors. These hurts could be from words that were misinterpreted, something done against you, circumstances, or lies that were told to you that you believed. Why else would you be damaging your body unless you felt you deserved it or that you were not enough?

I realized that I became "damaged freight" when I was 14 months old. I almost died as a toddler of dehydration. I heard about the incident my whole life, but I was misinterpreting what was said. I took it as a bad thing I did. I believed that I caused my family pain. I thought I actually had control over my life at that age. I should have stopped it. I was living my life as if it was my fault. This led me to believe that I deserved to be punished. The day that I realized that it wasn't my fault, I actually saw myself as a young child screaming, "It's not my fault!" My eyes were opened to the pain that I was carrying around in my life causing me to live from a position of woundedness and deserving punishment. As a young child under the age of five, the influential years, I became damaged. I felt worthless. I felt unloved…so since I felt like that, then that meant that I was.

2. Do you feel that you are responding to past hurts? Why/why not?

_____

_____

_____

3. When have you ever felt "crushed in spirit"? (Psalm 34:18)

_____

_____

_____

4. What hurts/wounds of your past are you beginning to feel? Ask God to reveal them to you.

   _____

   _____

   _____

5. What wounds do you need to surrender to God? What wounds do you believe are too big for God to heal?

   _____

   _____

   _____

6. What will God do with those hurts? (see Psalm 34:18)

   _____

   _____

   _____

7. When do you think you became damaged freight?

   _____

   _____

   _____

The mind is satan's playing field. He takes the condemning words and actions of others, along with his lies, and leads you into condemning behaviors. He even wants you to blame God for all the hurts in your life. In one of my pastor's sermons, he said that some people put the face of all the people that hurt you, those that played God in your life, onto the face of God, therefore leading them to blaming Him. Healing isn't about blaming. Don't listen to satan. It isn't God's fault. It isn't your fault.

> The mind is satan's playing field. He takes the condemning words and actions of others, along with his lies, and leads you into condemning behaviors.

Don't be discouraged. Your hope lies in the healing of the hurts of the past. Rest assured, God provided the cure in the healing power of His Son, Jesus Christ, your Savior.

The following shows how the original wound in your life births a food stronghold.

Birth of the Food Stronghold

1. Original wound, damaged freight (feeling rejected, unloved, worthless)
2. Regain position, by perfect performance…yet never good enough, numb the pain of reality
3. The behavior is born…first diet, first controlling of food and body…this I can control
4. Behavior begins to control you and you are now out of control (anorexia, bulimia, compulsive overeating is birthed)
5. Desperate State
6. Choice…healing of the initial wound
7. Freedom

I am living proof that there is a light at the end of the tunnel, and it is Jesus. Follow His light to freedom.

Reaching royalty wounds

- Begin today to write your life story.
    You are a princess or prince. Begin the story, "Once upon a time there lived a princess/prince named _____ (insert your name), who was created by God. God rejoiced over _____ (your name) with singing. This princess lived in a kingdom with…
    - People in your life
    - Include the feelings of this princess/prince
    - Give this princess/prince a voice in the different situations that she/he was faced with.

- End the story with the present moment and the desires of the princess'/prince's heart…how she/he really wants the story of his or her life to be
- Pray through this, cry through this, be the princess or prince....

This may be a difficult task for you as you look over your life and begin to uncover emotions. Give yourself grace. Take your time. Remember, God is with you through this. I did this and it really opened up my eyes, not only to the wounds in my life, but to a loving, comforting God who wants me to become the princess which He created me to be.

> "Through the heart's wound, I see its secret."
> -Bernard of Clairvaux (Eldredge, 118)

> "Through the heart's wound, I see its secret."
> -Bernard of Clairvaux

Day 5: Healing the Brokenhearted

1. When have you felt you have been judged or condemned?

   _____
   _____
   _____

2. Refer to Romans 8:1 and John 3:17-18. Does Jesus condemn you? Is Jesus bigger than those who may have hurt you in the past or those lies that you believe?

   _____
   _____
   _____

78 / Weightless: Flying Free

> You no longer have to act condemned, because in Jesus Christ you are not condemned.

You no longer have to act condemned, because in Jesus Christ you are not condemned. We all have wounds, and we have all been hurt, and that is exactly how Jesus wants you to come to Him. He wants you to come as you are. God chose you; He predestined you to be adopted as His daughter/son. "He predestined us to be adopted as His sons through Jesus Christ, in accordance with His pleasure and will— to the praise of His glorious grace, which He has freely given us in the One He loves" (Ephesians 1:5-6).

3. How do you feel that you have been adopted into God's family?

_____

_____

_____

A great example of adoption in the Bible is from the Old Testament story of Mephibosheth and his "adoption." Read the account from 2 Samuel 9:7-8 and answer the following questions.

4. How did Mephibosheth describe himself?

_____

_____

_____

5. Have you ever felt like a "dead dog"? If so, when and why?

_____

_____

_____

6. How did David treat him?

_____
_____
_____

Mephibosheth was amazed that he was "noticed". It seems to me that he never thought he deserved to be acknowledged.

7. When have you felt unnoticed? Have you ever felt undeserving of acknowledgement?

_____
_____
_____

God notices and accepts you...no matter what. Mephibosheth was injured, yet David adopted him into his family, as it was customary for a new king to take care of the family members of the previous king. Just as Mephibosheth was adopted into David's family, God allows us, through Jesus, to be adopted into His family.

> **God notices and accepts you...no matter what.**

8. If God is so gracious, how can you be gracious to yourself? Are you worth it?

_____
_____
_____

9. Jesus has come to heal your broken heart and your wounds (Psalm 147:3). What difference can that make in your life?

_____
_____
_____

Nothing has the power to heal, to change, to remove pain—just God. God is all-powerful and you have to put your pain and hurts in His hands. Jesus has come to heal the brokenhearted. I used food to heal the pain, when instead I was just numbing it. Trust and believe that He will heal the pain. He can't change your past, He can't change any of the pain or hurts you experienced, but He can change your reaction to it after He heals the wounds. Bring your hurts to the cross and trust that they will be healed because God said so.

Food for Thought

• Jesus' Prayer Box

Jesus wants your hurts, your wounds, and your prayers. When you give them to Him, He takes them as a gift. In my journaling time, I draw a box. I put a big cross in the center for the ribbon, representing Jesus, which divides the box into quarters. I then place a big bow on top. In each square I write my prayers, my hurts, my worries, and give them to Jesus as a gift. Fill in the box with your prayers and present them to Jesus.

Memory Verses

"He heals the brokenhearted and binds up their wounds."
Psalm 147:3

*"Therefore, there is now no condemnation for those
who are in Christ Jesus."*
Romans 8:1

Closing Prayer

Dear Lord, Thank You for adopting me into Your family. Your Son was crucified for me, so I no longer have to crucify myself. I can stand tall in Your name because You stand tall for me. I am Your child now, as You saved me from myself. Thank You for healing my wounds as I turn them over to You. Please give me strength as I let go of this food stronghold. In Jesus' name I pray.

Flying Forward

- Memorize Psalm 147:3 and Romans 8:1
- Read through next week's study and complete each day's questions throughout the week.

Week 6

The Promises And Lies of Food

> *"Then Jesus declared, 'I am the bread of life. He who comes to me will never go hungry, and He who believes in Me will never be thirsty.'"*
> John 6:35
>
> ## Opening Prayer
>
> Dear Lord, I come before You ready to uncover what lies beneath the food stronghold in my life. Reveal to me the triggers and the emotions behind it. Help me to draw on Your power that You demonstrated on the cross. Thank You that You satisfy all those empty places in my life. In Jesus' name I pray.
>
> ## Truth
>
> God is the only One who fully satisfies.

Day 1: God's Food

When no one would listen…food was there.
When not feeling loved…food was there.
When the loneliness was deafening…food was there.
I felt so empty, yet at times so full…so full of food. Why couldn't I get enough? Why couldn't I get enough of food? Why couldn't I be thinner? I always wanted more. We all hunger after something, what do you hunger after?

My biggest struggle during the bulimic years was never getting enough—enough of a good time, enough of a laugh, enough of happiness, enough of a delicious "forbidden" food. When I found the laugh, the happiness, the food, I held onto that moment for life, especially the food. When I would taste something that was so good, I couldn't stop. What was it that I really wanted? It really wasn't the food. It was the "good" feeling, the "good" taste of life. I was in such pain for so long that when I experienced anything that felt or tasted good I could never get enough. Food would never be able to fill the void that I had inside. Nothing could ever fill that void I had. I was like a cup with a hole in it. You can fill the cup, temporarily with water, but it will never be full.

When I was growing up, I was starving for attention. I tried to be the good girl, the perfect child…but it was never enough. Since whatever I did was never enough, it meant that I was not enough. I went from performance to controlling my appearance. Well, that still wasn't enough.

> **When I was growing up, I was starving for attention.**

1. When have you ever felt "not enough"? Describe.

   _____
   _____
   _____

2. What are some of those "voids" in your life? How does your stronghold try to fill them? Does it ever really work?

   _____
   _____
   _____

When God shed light on the truth that "just being Joni was enough", that was the day I had enough, had enough of the bulimia. I finally found the only person that could fill all the empty spaces in my life that I was trying to fill with food. Until I tried Jesus out, to see if He could fill my emptiness, it didn't make sense. It was true. I tried it all and nothing could or would ever fill my cup. Are you ready to make Him enough?

3. What happens in your life if you earnestly seek God? (Psalm 63:1,5)

   _____
   _____
   _____

4. What steps do you need to take to have your soul fully satisfied?

_____

_____

_____

5. Read Matthew 5:6. What will be the results in your life if you "...hunger and thirst after righteousness (uprightness and right standing with God)..." (Amplified Bible)?

_____

_____

_____

> When you spend your time trying to fill a void with food, that only God is able to fill, you will never be able to fill it;

When you spend your time trying to fill a void with food, that only God is able to fill, you will never be able to fill it; therefore you will never be able to stop eating…giving birth to a binge. I truly believed that food was able to fill all my emptiness. I wasn't able to stop the cycle, once I started, because the bulimia would never be able to fill that empty spot. Begin today to eat of the only real food that satisfies…, "Taste and see that the Lord is good..." (Psalm 34:8) and you will be truly blessed.

Day 2: God is All-Powerful

Your focus may be on food, but that isn't where the problem lies. It is not about the food. The answer lies beneath why you use food. If you have ever tried any diet, you are aware that the focus is always on the food…what you can or cannot eat. I remember my dieting days; they were spent thinking about food and the number on the scale. There is no freedom there if your concentration is always on food. The focus is always on the management of the behavior. Freedom from the behavior is permanent only when the hurts and wounds, which the stronghold is covering, are healed. If the root is not taken care of then the behavior will never change. That is why fad diets do not work. They provide immediate results, but not lasting ones. This week we will begin to analyze the food diary...the circumstances and emotions that trigger you into a food stronghold.

A trigger is defined as a stimulus that sets off an action, process, or series of events (Encarta). Comparing a trigger to a gun—a gun will only release the bullet after the trigger is pulled. The trigger exists, but it does not go off by itself, someone has to pull it. It is the same with the triggers in your life that cause you to fall. Those circumstances, those feelings, those people—that push your buttons—and the only way to react is in your stronghold—so you believe. Triggers will not go away. You will be faced with these all your life. You have no control when they will come. The only control over them that you do have is your reaction to them. Is your only option to pull the trigger? What are you to do with those intense emotions that are released after the triggering event?

Your reaction is related to the power you believe the trigger has. What power does it really have? What power does food really have? It may seem like it has a lot, but a gun just sitting there left untouched has no power to kill, only the one who handles the gun has the power to decide how to use it.

> **A trigger is defined as a stimulus that sets off an action, process, or series of events (Encarta).**

1. How do you feel when you are faced with an unwelcomed circumstance? What is your first reaction?

   _____

   _____

   _____

2. How much power does a trigger "appear" to have in the moment?

   _____

   _____

   _____

86 / *Weightless: Flying Free*

Read the account of David and Goliath in 1 Samuel 17:1-58. Goliath is described as a man who is 9 feet tall and girded in 125 pounds of armor and holding a 15-pound spear. David is described as "just a boy" with a slingshot.

3. Who "appears" to be stronger?

   _____
   _____
   _____

4. Why was David so confident in fighting Goliath? (see vs.37)

   _____
   _____
   _____

5. How was David able to confront and destroy Goliath? (1 Samuel 17:37,45-47)

   _____
   _____
   _____

6. Who really is stronger?

   _____
   _____
   _____

7. When are you the strongest according to Ephesians 6:9-10?

   _____
   _____
   _____

8. Where does the real power lie and whose battle is it?

_____

_____

_____

> **God is the only One who fully satisfies.**

God is bigger than the circumstances in your life. You lose control when you look at the triggering event as being bigger than God. God is aware of that trial that you are facing. He wants you to trust Him in the midst of it, even when you can't see the light at the end of the tunnel. He doesn't want the worries of tomorrow to burden the joys of today. Riding through the painful emotions is very hard. Facing the consequences of sin is a lot harder.

Day 3: Triggers

One of the characteristics of those who suffer in a food stronghold is perfectionism. "Perfectionism" would trigger me into the behavior. If I made a mistake—I would eat. If I couldn't do something perfectly—I would eat. If my house, my clothes, my hair, my body wasn't perfect—I would eat. I could never win. I was fighting a losing battle. We tend to give our triggers life and control. I gave my triggers an identity. Once I visualized a trigger as a stuffed animal standing in my kitchen unable to move. What power did this stuffed ball of fur have to make me eat or not eat? I could crush it like a bug, yet I gave it life. This just made me laugh. We think we have no power because we give things, situations, emotions, etc...such power to control us. In the process of trying to control we have actually lost control.

> **One of the characteristics of those who suffer in a food stronghold is perfectionism.**

1. What/Who are the "Goliaths" in your life that you give power to?

_____

_____

_____

2. Look over your food diary. Is there a specific time of day that you are most prone to your eating behavior? Note the times when you were drawn to your food stronghold.

   _____

   _____

   _____

3. What foods trigger the behavior?

   _____

   _____

   _____

4. What were the circumstances that drove you to practice your stronghold?

   _____

   _____

   _____

5. Is there a pattern of triggering events or people?

   _____

   _____

   _____

6. What emotions triggered your reaction? Fill in the blank with the emotion (some have been provided).

   I intake/restrict food when I am _____.

Afraid	Frustrated	Overwhelmed
Angry	Guilty	Peaceful
Anxious	Happy	Rejected
Bored	Hurt	Sad
Confused	Joyful	Tired
Discouraged	Lonely	Worried

7. What power do your triggers have in light of the story of David and Goliath? What is available to you when you are faced with a trigger?

_____

_____

_____

8. Whose battle is it when you are faced with a trigger? (1 Samuel 17:47)

_____

_____

_____

As a child of God, adopted into His kingdom, you have free access to God's power at the moment you are faced with a trigger. The same power that God used in creating the world is the same power He uses to answer our simple prayers. Everything God allows requires no effort on His part. If He can hold the sun in the sky, He can enable you to face a temptation without succumbing to the pressure. Believe that God's power in you is far greater than the power of a trigger or temptation.

It may not feel like it in the moment, but choose to believe it. "He who is in you is greater than He who is in the World" (1 John 4:4). God is always with you. You have to believe this and call on Him in order to experience His amazing power. You do not need to struggle on your own. "He gives strength to the weary and increases the power of the weak" (Isaiah 40:29). Draw on God's power to overcome. You don't have to give power to the look, power to the size, power to the _____. Allow God to have the power because He is the One who has the power.

> As a child of God, adopted into His kingdom, you have free access to God's power at the moment you are faced with a trigger.

Day 4: Free to Feel

I used food and the bulimia as a mask over my emotions. I remember the fear that overtook me when I would just try to feel an emotion. I pictured myself as a balloon that was ready to pop and if I even tried to "feel," my balloon would pop and there would be pieces of Joni all over the place. I believed the lie that I would explode if I allowed myself to feel. I did not want to feel me. That is why I did not like to feel full after I ate.

1. Fill in the following statements.

    - After I eat a meal I feel _____.
    - When my clothes are too tight I feel _____.
    - When I see the number on the scale I feel _____.
    - When I see someone who has what I desire (physically) I feel _____.

2. What emotions do you fear? Why?

    _____
    _____
    _____

3. What do you fear as you begin to uncover what lies beneath the food issues in your life?

    _____
    _____
    _____

4. What power do you give an emotion?

    _____
    _____
    _____

When emotions were too strong to deal with, food was right there to mask the feelings. When someone made me angry, food was there to take my side. When I was overwhelmed, food was there to quiet my soul. When I was alone, food was right there to keep me company. When I was bored, food gave me something to do. When I wanted to be loved, food would love me. When I needed an identity, I was Joni the bulimic. These were all lies. A food stronghold is a lie. It never delivers on its promises.

> When emotions were too strong to deal with, food was right there to mask the feelings.

5. Refer back to your answers to question 6, on Day 3 of this week. Which emotions do you consider "good" and which are considered "bad" in your life? Which emotions do you tend to stuff?

_____

_____

_____

6. What messages, "lies," are you receiving when you are triggered? What are food and/or the behavior telling you? For example, "No one loves me; I shouldn't be happy; I can't deal with this....".

_____

_____

_____

The food or the behavior is used as a response to an emotion, void, or circumstance. Satan wants you to believe that food or the behavior can heal your heart, cover your wounds, and fill your voids. He also wants you to fear your emotions. I believed that I shouldn't feel the negative emotions of anger, frustration, loneliness.... Emotions are just emotions. I would numb the "bad" ones and feel the "good" ones. I would even punish myself with food if I was feeling too good. I was afraid to feel. The shortest scripture is John 11:35, "Jesus wept." If Jesus cried, then it is okay for me to cry. Jesus has felt every emotion that you will ever feel. Today, I find comfort in my

> Jesus has felt every emotion that you will ever feel.

God and He replaces the "lies" with His truths, so there is no room for food. It took time to trust that God's Word was enough and that He could truly comfort me in those struggling moments. As I grew in my relationship with the Lord, I learned that I could trust Him and that He was always true to His Word.

In this life you will be faced with all emotions, as you were made as a "feeling" being. God's Word is filled with healthy responses, instead of the response of a food stronghold, when you are faced with those powerful emotions that feel as if they will overtake you.

7. Take the answers from question 6 and search the scriptures for God's response, God's answers. He always offers a solution and comfort. As you step out in faith and do what God says about a certain matter, then you will reap the benefits and blessings. God's promises are true.

For example:

You Say	God Says
Nobody loves me	I love you (John 3:16; 3:13-34)
I am all alone	I will never leave you (Hebrews 13:5)
I am anxious	I give you peace (Philippians 4:6-7)
I can't do it	You can do all things (Philippians 4:13)

When it comes to people who trigger those painful emotions, forgiveness is the road to peace.

Day 5: Jesus Satisfies

1. What does Jesus promise you? (John 6:35)

___

___

___

The Promises And Lies of Food / 93

2. How is Jesus and God's power "enough" for you, as you face the triggers and emotions in your life?

_____

_____

_____

You have been spending your time covering your emotions with the abuse of food. As your blanket of protection is being lifted, a slew of emotions will be exposed. Triggers and the emotions do not have the power to destroy, but it sure feels like they do. What are you to do with these new feelings that become so overwhelming? What is going to replace your security blanket? You feel so full, yet so empty.

> **You have been spending your time covering your emotions with the abuse of food**

3. Who has the ability to fill you completely as explained in John 6:35?

_____

_____

_____

4. What step do you need to take in order to be filled, with the true bread of life?

_____

_____

_____

5. Do you believe that Jesus is enough to fill the voids that food and the behavior is currently filling? Explain.

_____

_____

_____

6. How are you able to confront and destroy the power of a trigger?

   _____
   _____
   _____

7. Refer back to the triggers, the Goliaths, in your life. Picture one of your "Goliaths" in your mind. Now imagine Jesus standing next to this Goliath.

   - Who is bigger?

     _____
     _____
     _____

   - If Jesus and Goliath showed up at the same time, whose hand would you take?

     _____
     _____
     _____

   - Where will Goliath lead you?

     _____
     _____
     _____

   - Where will Jesus lead you and what will He provide for you?

     _____
     _____
     _____

8. Are you willing to allow Jesus to take all Goliath's power away? Do you believe Jesus is able?

___

9. Where will you get your strength according to Philippians 4:13?

___

10. What does Jesus offer you in John 14:27?

___

So...what are you to do with your triggers?

Food for Thought

"Without God you will never feel complete. God is the only One who can satisfy your deep-seated longings. God is the source of our peace" (Stanley, Finding Peace, 12).

Memory Verse

"Then Jesus declared, 'I am the bread of life. He who comes to me will never go hungry, and he who believes in me will never be thirsty.'"
John 6:35

Closing Prayer

Dear Lord, Thank You for being bigger than the Goliaths in my life. Strengthen me with Your power when I am faced with these triggers. Thank You for providing Your Son to rescue me immediately from the power of a trigger, and for being "enough" to satisfy all of my inner hungers. In Jesus' name I pray.

Flying Forward

- Memorize John 6:35
- After labeling those triggers (emotions, people, circumstances), which cause you to respond in an unhealthy manner, find scriptures that speak truth to these areas. Write the scriptures on an index card and keep them visible and read them immediately after being triggered.
- Read through next week's study and complete each day's questions throughout the week.

Week 7

I Do Have A Choice

"Submit yourselves, then, to God. Resist the devil, and He will flee from you. Come near to God and He will come near to you."
James 4:7-8a

Opening Prayer

Dear Lord, Help me to make You my first choice in everything. Give me the strength to overcome the power of temptation in my life. Show me what is really going on Lord. Where am I hurting? What am I trying to feed or starve? Please come into me and show me the wounds and heal them. In Jesus' name I pray.

Truth

God is always the perfect choice.

> God is always the perfect choice.

Power of a Trigger

As I sit before the ocean, a sudden sense of peace sweeps over me. How can a body of water so vast, so powerful, be so peaceful? The roars of the waves are soothing to my soul…so uncontrollable, yet controlled. Lord, you are the sea; you are so vast, so powerful, yet soothing to my soul, while I am so out of control. I am able to rest in you because you are in control.

The food stronghold in my life was like a wave, a tidal wave, a response to factors outside of myself. Just like the ocean responds to the sun and the moon, I responded to my triggers. A trigger in my life would be the beginning of a tidal wave. It was automatic. There would be no turning back. Once the wave began to form, it wouldn't end until it broke and came crashing down, crashing down into the binge/purge cycle. I allowed the trigger to give me permission to practice bulimia, because I thought that was my only choice, my only option, my only relief. The life that I had been trying to control was really out of control.

> I was led to believe...deceived... that my only option was to binge, purge, or starve myself.

After a wave crashes on the shore it becomes a peaceful pool of water. Right before it crashes is when you do have a choice. The wave becomes a wave as soon as it is triggered. There is no turning back. When I was triggered, temptation entered and I couldn't resist. I also felt that there was no turning back. My only choice was to go to the eating behavior. I was led to believe...deceived... that my only option was to binge, purge, or starve myself. How else was I to respond? I never knew that I had another choice. Do you realize that you have a choice not to choose?

Day 1: Choice to Choose

I would allow anything in my life to give me permission to eat. The bottom line was that my mind was already made up that I would go to food. Food was all that I wanted, and there was no room for negotiation. I had to run to what I only knew to be true...food and bulimia. It was my only relief. Food provided two choices...abuse it or refuse it. I was on a mission and I didn't truly want a way out. Then one day I realized…I do have a choice…and food wasn't it. To realize that I did have another option that God was there with me, gave me the desire to choose God. Why live as a product of a bad choice when you are a product of a good choice: God's chosen.

> I would begin many days exhausted, mentally and physically, because of a poor choice(s) I had made the day before.

I would begin many days exhausted, mentally and physically, because of a poor choice(s) I had made the day before. Every day provided an opportunity to make the right choices, despite how I felt. With my focus on the Lord and not on me, I was able to make the right choices.

1. What do you base your joy on for the day?

   _____

   _____

   _____

2. What reason does Psalm 118:24 give for rejoicing?

   _____

   _____

   _____

3. When are you to rejoice according to Philippians 4:4, and how is that possible?

   _____
   _____
   _____

4. Read Psalm 90:12. Answer the following in light of this verse.

- If you only had today, what would you do differently than yesterday?

   _____
   _____
   _____

- If you only had today, what different choices would you make in the following areas of your life:
    - Physically (in the way that you care for yourself)

      _____
      _____
      _____

    - Spiritually

      _____
      _____
      _____

    - Emotionally

      _____
      _____
      _____

5. If you only had today, would you continue in the eating behavior? Explain.

   _____
   _____
   _____

6. Do you believe that right now you can "choose" to "not choose" food as your stronghold, and be totally free? How does this make you feel?

   _____
   _____
   _____

> **When I was in the midst of the stronghold I would cry out, "why can't I stop?"**

When I was in the midst of the stronghold I would cry out, "why can't I stop?" I really believed that I couldn't stop, until the day that God pointed out to me, "why won't you stop?" You do have the freedom to choose how you will respond to a trigger or triggering event.

7. Fill in the following statement using your responses from Week 5, Day 3, and any more that you may think of, and repeat it to yourself.

   I do not have to intake/restrict food when I am _____.

Afraid	Frustrated	Overwhelmed
Angry	Guilty	Peaceful
Anxious	Happy	Rejected
Bored	Hurt	Sad
Confused	Joyful	Tired
Discouraged	Lonely	Worried

   What are you to do instead of practicing the behavior in order to break the habit? I had a list of healthy alternative behaviors that I could go to instead of going to the food, in order to break the habit. It would give me time before the emotions had a chance to set in. Sometimes the only option and the most effective thing you can do is to "flee" (1 Corinthians 10:14) from the scene. This allows you time to regroup so you can stop and think clearly. I know what it feels like in the heat of the moment, and even when I prayed and asked God to strengthen me, it wouldn't seem like enough. As I grew in my faith, God became enough. I first had to begin to replace my unhealthy behaviors with healthy ones. In this process I rediscovered and discovered what I liked to do and how to take care of myself.

> I first had to begin to replace my unhealthy behaviors with healthy ones.

8. Make a list of feasible alternatives that you could go to at that moment you are triggered, and have them handy. Fill in the following blank with those.

   I will _____ when I am faced with the temptation to run to a food stronghold.

Bike ride	Flee	Listen to music	Read a book
Count to ten	Go for a walk	Phone a friend	Take a bath
Cry	Journal	Pray	Watch a movie

Don't allow a poor choice to ruin a day that the Lord has given you to live in freedom. You are allowed to enjoy today because "this is the day the Lord has made; let us rejoice and be glad in it" (Psalm 118:24).

Day 2: Waves of Temptation

Even though God gave us the free will to choose, why is it so hard to make the right choice? You now have a list of alternative behaviors to replace the food stronghold, but what happens when you are faced with making the right choice and you choose the wrong one? What gets in the way? Temptation. Temptation is a craving or desire for something, especially something thought wrong. Temptation is real.

1. Who does 1 Corinthians 10:13 say experiences temptation?

   _____

   _____

   _____

2. Read the account of Adam and Eve in Genesis 3:1-7. What choice did Eve have? Why do you think it was so hard for her to choose not to eat the forbidden fruit?

_____

_____

_____

3. Read 2 Samuel 11:1-4. What choice did David have when he saw Bathsheba?

_____

_____

_____

4. When did Eve's and David's temptation begin? Why do you think they succumbed to sin?

_____

_____

_____

5. How do you feel when you are faced with the opportunity to practice your eating behavior? Is the temptation real?

_____

_____

_____

> **Food always allowed a choice. I could abuse or refuse it. I had the power.**

Food always allowed a choice. I could abuse or refuse it. I had the power. Food was right there and "choice" was standing right next to it. When I placed Christ in-between the food and my choice, the right choice was easy, but when I went directly from the trigger to the food, I would begin the spiral downward. In Christ, we all have a choice. You have a choice to choose Him or not. You have a choice to choose the eating behavior. You do have a choice right after the triggering event. Take ownership of how you will react.

Read 1 Corinthians 10:13 and answer the following.

6. What does God say He will do when you are tempted to practice your stronghold? Do you believe this truth? Explain.

   _____

   _____

   _____

7. Why will God not allow you to be tempted beyond what you are able to bear? How does the truth that God will not give you more than you can bear help you when you are standing face to face with the burning desire to go to the food stronghold?

   _____

   _____

   _____

8. How would God's faithfulness help you in times of temptation?

   _____

   _____

   _____

9. What will God provide for you when you are faced with a trigger and the choice? How does this affect the choice you will make when you are feeling helpless?

   _____

   _____

   _____

Day 3: Sinful Nature

When Eve took the first bite, there was no turning back. The process began. The desire had already taken root in her, which made it easier for her to succumb to the serpent's craftiness.

James 1:13-15 describes the steps one takes from a trigger to the practice of the eating behavior. Read this scripture and answer the following.

> When Eve took the first bite, there was no turning back.

1. What happens right after one is tempted?

   _____
   _____
   _____

2. What happens after desire is conceived?

   _____
   _____
   _____

3. When does the desire for you to go to the eating behavior first strike?

   _____
   _____
   _____

4. What triggers "drag you away and entice you" to practice the eating behavior?

   _____
   _____
   _____

5. At what point in this cycle are you offered the opportunity to make a choice?

   _____

   _____

   _____

6. *"...But if you do not do what is right, sin is crouching at your door; it desires to have you, but you must master it"* (Genesis 4:7). What is waiting for you when you make the unhealthy choice? How can you become master over the food stronghold when it comes "crouching at your door"?

   _____

   _____

   _____

7. What do you desire from the practicing of the stronghold?

   _____

   _____

   _____

> When I was told, as a new believer, that the food stronghold in my life was a sin, it scared me and made me angry. I did not see it as a sin pattern in my life

Sin, is defined as "self-will, characterized by an attitude of active rebellion or passive indifference" (Campus). Sin enslaves you and destroys. When I was told, as a new believer, that the food stronghold in my life was a sin, it scared me and made me angry. I did not see it as a sin pattern in my life. I was in such pain, and I didn't think I was doing anything deliberate. I felt like a prisoner. As I searched the scriptures I realized that sin was separation from God. In those moments of binging and purging, I was separated from God. It was my sin nature. The sinful nature is whatever I desire that is against what God desires for me. He does not want you or me to be consumed with food or a number on a scale. He wants you to be consumed with Him, and what He desires. I have learned many things about myself through my recovery, and the biggest lesson learned has been that I was my own worst enemy. But why did I continue in this behavior if I hated it so much?

Romans 7:15-20 explains this... *"I do not understand what I do. For what I want to do I do not do, but what I hate I do. And if I do what I do not want to do, I agree that the law is good. As it is, it is no longer I myself who do it, but it is sin living in me. I know that nothing good lives in me, that is, in my sinful nature. For I have the desire to do what is good, but I cannot carry it out. For what I do is not the good I want to do; no, the evil I do not want to do–this I keep on doing. Now if I do what I do not want to do, it is no longer I who do it, but it is sin living in me that does it."*

I just love looking at this scripture and seeing all of the "dos" and "don'ts". It really describes the confusion that is in my mind when I am overwhelmed with emotions and not knowing what to do with them. I know what I should do, but *"...when I want to do good, evil is right there with me"* (Romans 7:21), yet I end up succumbing to the temptation.

8. How does Romans 7 relate to your experience when faced with the decision whether or not to choose the eating behavior?

_____

_____

_____

> **It all starts in our minds. It is where you set yourself up to fail...**

It all starts in our minds. It is where you set yourself up to fail...giving in to your natural desires, what you really want to do. Why do you follow through when you know the outcome? Who are you really trying to fool? How do you break this cycle? How do you not listen to the lies, the tricks, and the deceit? The solution is twofold. Realize it is the sin in you, and you need to submit (yield, to surrender, to give in [Encarta]) to God and rebuke the evil one (satan has other plans which we'll discuss in Day 4). The food has no power. Your mind is driving you to complete the task. Also, try to then picture the outcome in your head. How will you feel if you carry out your plan? Is it really worth it?

Refer to James 4:7-8 as you answer the following questions.

9. In what ways will submission to God help you to resist the temptation to practice the eating behavior? What is the only way that you are able to resist it?

_____

_____

_____

10. What will God do for you if you are to submit and draw near to Him?

_____

_____

_____

11. Do you believe this is enough to overcome your eating stronghold?

_____

_____

_____

I have to pursue my God daily, not only because I suffered in a food stronghold, but also because I am human. God knows that my spirit is willing, yet I am weak.

12. Matthew 26:41 also gives a solution to fighting temptation.

- How can you prepare yourself against the temptation to practice a food stronghold?

_____

_____

_____

- Will you be faced with temptation even though you don't want to fall into it?

- What is your only protection against temptation?

> Don't be so surprised by temptation, even Jesus faced it.

There were many times that I knew that I would be faced with a tempting situation that would push my buttons. I knew that I would have to choose God, first, or I would have been defeated. Don't be so surprised by temptation, even Jesus faced it.

Day 4: Tricks of the Trade

When I deviate from the things that I know I should be doing in order to protect myself from temptation, I begin to downsize and lose my focus. It only takes one false move to lead to destruction. Let's consider those little compromises... those little tricks that deceive us into an action.

1. Who tempts, according to Matthew 5:1?

2. How is satan described in 1 Peter 5:7? What does he want to do to you? How does that make you feel?

3. What was satan to Jesus in Matthew 16:23? Does this describe him in your life?

_____

_____

_____

Satan, the great deceiver and crafty serpent, has one goal in mind, and that is to devour, to destroy. Satan uses you. He wants you to fail, and after you fail he rejoices as the winner. Don't you feel devoured in the food stronghold? After every trigger and temptation, satan led me to believe that there was no hope, no way out...so my only option was to choose what I knew worked. He is on a mission. Satan always meets you at the right place, the right time, when you are most vulnerable. The subtleties of satan and his enticement—making it seem okay to put your foot in the forbidden waters. As in the Garden, right before Eve took the fruit, she saw that it was pleasing to the eye. Isn't that how satan always works? He presents himself in something that looks good.

> Satan, the great deceiver and crafty serpent, has one goal in mind, and that is to devour, to destroy. Satan uses you.

Matthew 4:1-11 describes the temptations of Jesus by satan. Each time, satan brought Jesus to a place where He would be most vulnerable. Before the first temptation, Jesus had just fasted for forty days and was very hungry. This is the place where satan showed up, the place where Jesus was most vulnerable.

4. What are those places where you are most vulnerable to running to the food stronghold?

_____

_____

_____

5. What are the foods that trigger you into the eating behavior?

_____

_____

_____

6. What are some of the "tricks" that satan uses to trick you into the eating behavior?

_____

_____

_____

I would purposely test myself, when I knew I was weak. I would go right to the temptation (food, situation), because down deep I really did want to succumb. I would subconsciously turn my head to the side, in rebellion, so I didn't have to look at God. I would purposely turn away, so I didn't have to face Him, because I knew that if I did I would not get what I thought I wanted. I knew the danger spots; I knew all the tricks in the book. It was at those times that satan was right there to feed the lie.

The lies begin with the evil one... "I'll just have one (knowing I would eat the whole bag), I'll buy the cookies for the kids (I really wanted them), I'll just go in the kitchen and get a glass of water (because there was something I wanted to eat in the refrigerator). The games we play to keep our stronghold! Who was I trying to fool...or who was trying to make me look like a fool?

In Joshua 23:6, Joshua was speaking to Israel to remind them of what God had done and what they were to do in order to move on, to succeed.

> The lies begin with the evil one... "I'll just have one (knowing I would eat the whole bag)

7. What were they to do and not to do?

_____

_____

_____

8. What are you to do in order to overcome?

_____
_____
_____

9. What does it mean to turn to the right or left?

_____
_____
_____

10. How do you compromise yourself by turning to the right or the left?

_____
_____
_____

11. What games do you play with the food stronghold?

_____
_____
_____

The company you keep influences the type of person you become. For the time being, stay away from those places where you know you will be tempted, those times that feed the behavior. Don't go where you know you will be pushed, if at all possible. You may have to sacrifice some things in order to keep from practicing the behavior. "'Everything is permissible'—but not everything is beneficial. 'Everything is permissible'—but not everything is constructive" (1 Corinthians 10:23). Don't test yourself when you are feeling weak. As soon as you begin to see the signs you need to run to Christ and get strength. Scripture tells us that we are to be alert and self-controlled. We are to always be prepared, be on the lookout, especially when we begin to think we have it all together.

> The company you keep influences the type of person you become.

12. In what areas of your life, that you do have control over, do you need to make some changes, just for the time being, in order for you to guard yourself against temptation?

_____

_____

_____

When I succumb to the temptation, I suffer in the long run. When right at my fingertips I can choose Christ, and instead I choose to do what hurts me. The enemy loves it.

What about those circumstances which you are unable to avoid (work situation, a person...)? When you have no choice and are in a triggering situation or faced with a triggering food, God always provides a solution; a way out (1 Corinthians 10:13). You do have the power to overcome...through Christ who gives you strength. Submit to God, rest in Him, and trust and believe, that when you are faced with a trigger or temptation, He will provide a way out. As your relationship with the Lord grows, you will begin to develop better habits that replace the old habits of the past, and be able to handle whatever comes your way. I never thought that I could ever have a bag of Oreos or any treat in my house, without me devouring it in one sitting. I laugh at the fact that I now have to throw out the Oreos, because they have become stale. Follow what Peter said in I Peter 1:13, *"Therefore, prepare your minds for action; be self-controlled; set your hope fully on the grace to be given you when Jesus Christ is revealed."* Close the door to satan and open the door to freedom.

Day 5: A Taste of Freedom

All you are familiar with is your stronghold. We all like familiar. Change isn't always welcomed, because we know that change means that you have to do something and face something that you fear. Isn't it change that gets the applause after you go through it? When you succumb to temptation and immediately go to your stronghold, you never have the opportunity to taste a

> **All you are familiar with is your stronghold. We all like familiar. Change isn't always welcomed...**

piece of freedom. What does it really feel like to "feel"? What does it really feel like to "make the right choice"? What does it really feel like to take care of my body in the right way? What does it really feel like to enjoy food? What does it really feel like to not deny myself nourishment? What does it really feel like to be free in Christ? What does it really feel like to overcome?

How will you ever know what freedom tastes like unless you allow an opening between the triggering event to your immediate response to go to food or to starve? What are you afraid of in that split second? What do you fear will happen if you don't choose your stronghold? What do you fear will happen that God won't be able to handle?

1. How do you think Jesus felt when He was faced with temptation? (Hebrews 2:18)

   _____
   _____
   _____

2. What did Jesus use to refute satan in His three confrontations with him? (Matthew 4:10-11)

   _____
   _____
   _____

3. What did satan end up doing?

   _____
   _____
   _____

4. How are you to overcome satan's attacks, using Jesus' example? Do you believe that God's Word is enough to combat temptation?

_____

_____

_____

Think about a food that you truly love the taste of. As soon as it hits your tongue your taste buds go wild. *How did you know that you actually liked this food? How did you know that it would taste good?* There has to be a first time that you tasted the food in order to realize that you liked it. It is the same with experiencing freedom. How do you know if you like it or not if you don't taste it? How can you think that "you will never be free" if you never allow the opportunity? There is always a small door of opportunity when it comes to making a choice. Are you ready to open that door, for a second, and just taste it?

I remember the first time, after a binge, that I was choosing not to purge. It was so very painful. It was so painful because I allowed fear to get the best of me. My biggest fear was that I would gain 100 pounds if I didn't purge. That really isn't true, that is impossible, but in my mind I truly believed it because I "felt" like I already gained the weight. I hated feeling full. What I really hated was feeling anything, especially my own skin. It was the hardest night of my life, but life changing. It was so freeing to wake up the next morning realizing that I didn't gain 100 pounds, but most of all I experienced what it felt like not to purge. I didn't realize how much "purging" really affected my body. I had a taste of "healthy", a taste of normal. I tasted hope. If I didn't walk out in faith, I would have never experienced the taste of freedom.

I allowed a "door of opportunity," a door of recovery to open up. I would never be the same again because I knew I had a choice. Just like a 50-degree sunny day in the middle of a cold winter. It is a glimmer of hope. Spring will come.

God is always offering hope in our lives, but we have to open the door.

> **I remember the first time, after a binge, that I was choosing not to purge. It was so very painful.**

5. Who will be with you when you open the door?

6. Why should you be confident in approaching Jesus when you are faced with temptation? (Hebrews 2:18)

7. Is Jesus able to handle your emotions at the time of the temptation? (Hebrews 4:15)

8. How does the truth that Jesus knows what you are going through, help you when you are faced with temptation?

Jesus has also supplied another solution in Luke 22:40. *"On reaching the place, He said to them, 'Pray that you will not fall into temptation.'"*

9. What did Jesus tell His disciples to do? Why?

10. What power does prayer have in your life?

_____

_____

_____

What is interesting about this passage is that Jesus was going to pray. Jesus prayed...a lot. After He prayed an angel appeared and strengthened Him. He prayed and received.

Reality is that you will be faced with temptation, and that God has provided solutions when you are faced with it. His own Son was even tempted, so He knows what you are going through. Jesus broke the power and the sting of satan. Satan may tempt, but Jesus overcame Him, so you can too.

> Reality is that you will be faced with temptation, and that God has provided solutions when you are faced with it.

Food for Thought

"Our strongest motivation will be the Person with whom we walk. Staying close to Him through constant communication, we receive a continual supply of strength to walk victoriously—in peace even as we walk through a war zone. We must walk with Christ step-by-step through this journey if we are to experience His protection, power, and a resulting passion in our lives. None of these three will be realities any other way. When we get close to Christ, the enemy will be defeated. Believe it. Act on it" (Moore, 86-87).

Memory Verse

"Submit yourselves, then, to God. Resist the devil, and he will flee from you. Come near to God and he will come near to you."
James 4:7-8a

Closing Prayer

Dear Lord, Thank You that You always supply a way out for me when I am faced with temptation. Provide for me healthy, alternative behaviors. Give me the strength to overcome the temptation to choose the food stronghold when faced with a trigger. In Jesus' name I pray.

Flying Forward

- Memorize James 4:7-8a
- Begin this week discovering the simple things in life that bring you joy, such as...
    - Take a walk with a friend
    - Just sit and be with God
    - Read a book
    - Take up a new sport/exercise
    - Try something that you have always wanted to but were afraid to
- Read through next week's study and complete each day's questions throughout the week.

Week 8

Responding As A Child Of God

> *"I am the vine; you are the branches. If a man remains in me and I in him, he will bear much fruit; apart from me you can do nothing."*
> John 15:5

Opening Prayer

Dear Lord, Fill me with the power of Your Spirit so I am able to produce the fruit that comes only from You. Thank you for the freedom that You provide as I remain in You. In Jesus' name I pray.

Truth

All things are possible for me, when I remain in Christ and plug into the power of the Holy Spirit.

> All things are possible for me, when I remain in Christ and plug into the power of the Holy Spirit.

> A child of God believes God's Word, trusts in the author and not in feelings...

A child of God believes God's Word, trusts in the author and not in feelings, draws strength from the Holy Spirit, and abides in Jesus Christ. If one is walking in these truths, he will tend to take appropriate action when triggered, rather than react by responding emotionally. Running to a food stronghold is a reaction to the feelings experienced.

There is no freedom in reacting in a negative manner. There is freedom in action. If God would have reacted to our sinful nature and gave us what we deserved, He would have never offered a solution. Instead, God took action; He acted out of His love and His grace (the infinite love, mercy, favor, and goodwill shown to humankind by God [Encarta]) and offered forgiveness through His Son.

I only knew to react. Reacting doesn't get you anywhere, except deeper in a hole of anger and bitterness. I realized the binging on food, the starving, and the purging, were my way of reacting to my pain. A food stronghold is the reaction, or response, to a wound, hurt, and pain. I thought that I was taking action, but that was a lie.

> A food stronghold is the reaction, or response, to a wound, hurt, and pain.

1. How are you supposed to respond now that you are feeling and facing hurts and emotions that have been covered by a food stronghold? The truth is that it isn't in the doing of something; it is in the going to the "someone." Do you tend to react or act?

   _____

   _____

   _____

2. Do you see the food stronghold in your life as a response?

   _____

   _____

   _____

Day 1: Drawing from the Source

There is a war raging inside of you between what your nature desires and what God desires. We all have a sinful nature. Satan lives and rules, so my natural tendencies are to go after what my sinful nature desires and to deal with things in my own way. God has promised forgiveness and eternity with Jesus. My destiny is sealed with Christ, but as long as I live in this body, on this earth, my nature will want to go after that which will lead me to destruction. As the Bible says, *"There is a way that seems right to a man, but in the end it leads to death"* (Proverbs 16:25). There is no need to be hard on yourself when the desire to starve, binge, or purge comes up. Take that desire to the Lord. Desires will remain, but it is your response to the desire that will determine the outcome.

> There is a war raging inside of you between what your nature desires and what God desires.

1. Since God is all-knowing, and He knows how you will be faced with temptation and trials, whom has He sent to help you? (John 14:16-18)

___

___

___

2. What are the roles of the Holy Spirit? (see also John 14:26)

___

___

___

3. Where does the Holy Spirit reside? What power is available to you at any time?

___

___

___

4. What does Romans 8:16 call you? How does the truth that God has not left you as an orphan, give you strength to face the food stronghold?

___

___

___

> **God has given us our own power source—the Holy Spirit.**

God has given us our own power source—the Holy Spirit. We are no longer orphans. The Holy Spirit is the one who makes it possible for you to live beyond yourself. Jesus is the ultimate Wound Healer. He understands all your emotions, whether rejection, loneliness, anger, etc. The Bible tells of Jesus' cries and tears (Hebrews 5:7). He knows pain since He suffered it firsthand. Jesus doesn't stop at just understanding. He provides the strength needed to face anything.

Food was my Holy Spirit. It served as my counselor, my friend, which lived inside me. It "helped" me when I was feeling anything I couldn't deal with. I was powerless. After receiving Jesus as my Savior and experiencing His power in my life, I found the hope and strength necessary to overcome. That power was in me, and I was able to draw from it at anytime. It is impossible to overcome anything by yourself. Plugging into the power was my choice.

5. What does it mean to you that you have this ultimate power source of the Holy Spirit living in you?

_____

_____

_____

6. In what ways is the Holy Spirit able to help you to overcome the eating behavior?

_____

_____

_____

7. What do you need to do in order to plug into this power?

_____

_____

_____

Rest in the arms of your Father. Accept His gifts of His Son and His Holy Spirit and walk in this power.

Day 2: Live by the Spirit

There are two trees planted at the curb of our beach house. One of the trees is flourishing; the other has struggled since the day it was planted. The healthy one just towers over the other tree. The little one will probably not make it. I was concerned about the trees in the first place because I thought the roots would eventually push up the sidewalk. My neighbor said that this wouldn't happen because they purposely planted fruitless fruit trees; their roots grow differently. What really caught my attention was when she said they are fruit trees that won't grow fruit. How am I like that tree? I become a fruit tree when I am planted in the Lord, but am I living like a fruitless one? No matter how beautiful or healthy this tree will be, it will never bear fruit. No matter how thin, or in shape, or beautiful I become, if I don't produce fruit, then what is the point? A perfect food plan, a perfect exercise plan, the perfect clothes…may produce the appearance of the perfect life. Why go after the fruit of the world when you can have the fruit of the Spirit. My fleshly goals of perfection in my appearance and performance will never give me fruit. Only Christ has that power. I want the fruit that Christ has to offer me.

> No matter how thin, or in shape, or beautiful I become, if I don't produce fruit, then what is the point?

1. List the fruit of the Spirit. How are they produced? (Galatians 5:22-25)

   _____
   _____
   _____

2. Which fruit do you possess now and which do you desire?

   _____
   _____
   _____

Responding As A Child Of God / 123

3. Refer to the list of the fruit from question 1. Fill in the following statement with each fruit of the Spirit. Which ones are you trying to find in a food stronghold?

   I **want** _____ from the food stronghold.

   I **get** _____ from the food stronghold.

4. Look over the above list. Which statements are true and which are false in your life?

   _____
   _____
   _____

5. What have you learned from the above exercise? What do you really want in your life compared to what you are getting?

   _____
   _____
   _____

   A major stumbling block in keeping me stuck in the behavior was that I was still seeking fruit from food. I wanted to believe that food could meet all my needs. Deep down I knew it was a lie, but what I really wanted was to satisfy my desires that were contrary to God's desires for me. The Bible calls this the sinful nature.

   > A major stumbling block in keeping me stuck in the behavior was that I was still seeking the fruit from food.

6. Refer to Romans 8:5-8. List the characteristics of someone who lives according to the sinful nature and someone who lives according to the Spirit.

   _____
   _____
   _____

7. What are some of your "natural" desires? Now consider which ones are of your sinful nature and which are of the Spirit. Where is your focus when you are seeking after what your nature desires? Complete the following example.

- If I desire a skinny body, my focus will be on _____.

- If I desire a healthy body, my focus will be on _____.

- If I desire freedom, my focus will be on _____.

8. What solution does Galatians 5:16 and verse 25 provide?

_____

_____

_____

> Do not let your emotions get in the way. It is hard to do what is right, that is why the Lord gave you the Holy Spirit.

Wherever your focus is, that is what will consume you. If your focus is on Christ and the prompting of the Holy Spirit, you will conquer those sinful desires. Do not let your emotions get in the way. It is hard to do what is right, that is why the Lord gave you the Holy Spirit. No matter how hard it may seem, believe in the power that resides inside you, draw from it, and run to the cross. Be proactive. *"Let us not become weary in doing good, for at the proper time we will reap a harvest if we do not give up"* (Galatians 6:9).

Day 3: Responding as a Child of God

1. What perks do you receive as a child of God? (Galatians 4:6-7)

_____

_____

_____

2. As a child of God, do you feel free? Explain.

_____

_____

_____

I am saved. God loves me. I am perfect in His sight, but where is my joy? Why am I not able to enjoy? How do I live now as a new creation, as an adopted child of our Lord, and not as a wounded child?

"Bulimia" was a big ball and chain that I dragged around, every day, everywhere I went. It was holding me back from experiencing the life that God had planned for me. I knew that God loved me and that I was perfect in His sight, but where was my joy? Why was I not able to enjoy? I was so stuck in food strongholds for so many years, that when I was set free of the behaviors I was not living as free.

I was living life on a mission, a mission to fix everything and everyone in my past and in the present, before I could totally enjoy my blessings. Since I was living my life still from a wounded position, I was not able to enjoy the joy of the Lord. I didn't allow myself to be happy until everything around me was fixed and I was perfect.

The song entitled *You Did That For Me* (Jonell Mosser/Pierce Pettis) is about Jesus dying for us…for me, for you. This song explains how Jesus did enough for the cost of all of our sins, by wearing the chains of the crucifixion, so you and I are able to just rest in the power of the cross and the punishment that He took. I realized that I was still wearing the chains, while I was trying to be free. Jesus gave His life, suffered in His death…all for me…so why did I still carry the burdens that Jesus set me free from and continue to be chained to the past? Didn't Jesus do enough for me? He was crucified, so why was I living a life that was crucifying me? Why was I still punishing myself? I was living like a prisoner who was holding the key to release the cell door.

3. What chains do you still wear that are getting in the way of you producing fruit?

   _____

   _____

   _____

4. Why do you think you need them?

   _____

   _____

   _____

5. If Jesus did enough for you, what is getting in the way of your surrendering your chains so you can be free?

   _____

   _____

   _____

> **You are free, because Christ has come to set you free.**

You are free, because Christ has come to set you free. When I finally realized that I was free…not because of who I was, or what I did, and even in my imperfections…was when I was able to rejoice in the Lord and able to respond as a child of the Father.

The saying WWJD is a reminder to think about What Would Jesus Do, when faced with a choice. You would have to know about Jesus in order to respond as He did. In order to respond as a child of God, you need to accept the truth that you are a child of God. How does a child of God respond? The secret lies in your acceptance of His grace and love for you. God is your father no matter what you believe or feel about yourself.

> *"All that Jesus did and said flowed out of His relationship with His Father. His sense of identity (who He was) was not based on His ministry (what He did), but just the reverse: He did what He did because He knew who He was"* (Intervarsity).

Responding As A Child Of God / 127

6. Refer to the above quote. Who is Jesus? With whom does He have a relationship? On what is His sense of identity based?

_____

_____

_____

7. Who does Galatians 4:6-7 say you are? On what is your sense of identity based?

_____

_____

_____

8. How would you live your day differently if you believed that...

- you are accepted?

    _____

    _____

    _____

- you are loved?

    _____

    _____

    _____

- you are chosen?

    _____

    _____

    _____

- you are free?

    _____

    _____

    _____

- you are not guilty?

9. How do you think a child of God responds when faced with the choice of practicing a food stronghold?

10. What would help you to respond as a child of God?

> **Perfect is not because of what you do; it is because of who you are in Christ. Jesus covers you with His perfection.**

As a child of God, you can live your day from a position of Perfect. It isn't perfect from a worldly perspective, but from God's perspective. You are perfect in His sight because you are His child. Perfect is not because of what you do; it is because of who you are in Christ. Jesus covers you with His perfection. My life's search for perfection has finally been found in the only place where it can be found—in my Savior.

Day 4: Falsely Accused

1. How would a wounded child, who feels condemned and unloved, tend to act?

I was forgiven by God and found "not guilty," but why did I continue to live as guilty, as a prisoner in my own skin? Recently, I watched a movie about the children of the Holocaust. After these precious children were released from the prisoners' camp, they were sent to a place where they were cared for and loved. Their first reactions always came from a position of fear. It was hard for them to accept love and to trust those who cared for them because of the mistreatment and the sorrow they experienced in the past. All they knew was abuse, so they responded to everything defensively and fearfully. They acted guilty, even though there was no crime. It took time for these children to trust and accept love from others. After I accepted Christ into my life, it took time for me to really grasp the love He had for me. It was too much too fathom. Because I felt so beaten, it was hard to accept this gift. I was not able to accept God's forgiveness or love—because I didn't feel perfect...yet.

Satan led me to believe that I could be and do all, just as he deceived Eve in the garden. *"For God knows that when you eat of it your eyes will be opened, and you will be like God, knowing good and evil"*(Genesis 3:5). He led Eve to believe that she could have it all and he did the same with me. Why would God find me perfect when I didn't feel perfect?

> Satan led me to believe that I could be and do all, just as he deceived Eve in the garden

I was listening to the condemning voice inside. I still felt that something was wrong with me, therefore I was always on the defense. I personalized and took to heart, every look, comment, or action. I was always on the lookout, just waiting for the one wrong…anything, which would stir all of my emotions. I would then pick myself apart, which would lead me into the binging, and then I would have to purge before I would explode. Satan had set me up with unreasonable expectations. He convinced me that I could meet all the expectations that I put on myself, and since I didn't, then I wasn't good enough...even for God.

- The lie—this is you, you will always struggle
- The lie—poor you, you are a victim
- The lie—you are not good enough—even for God

It would be at that point when I couldn't stand being in my own skin, so I would run to the food and the cycle would begin. The lies...you are bad, you are selfish, you are a failure, would fuel the behavior. What else was I supposed to do with all those lies? Since I felt worthless, condemned, and judged, then that meant that I was worthless, condemned, and judged. I was living from a position of guilty.

2. What does your condemning voice tell you?

___

___

___

3. Who is the master accuser in Revelation 12:9-10?

___

___

___

> **Jesus felt every emotion that is common to man, yet He never reacted to the emotions.**

Jesus felt every emotion that is common to man, yet He never reacted to the emotions. It doesn't matter if your emotions about something are justified. Satan wants you to stew in the pain. This is self-righteous pain, undeserved pain that you carry around and do not let go. He wants you to act as a victim. You have a choice to react or to act. Reacting is a step backwards, acting is a step forward. When living in the pain and living in the wounds, the only way to react is in an ineffective manner.

4. What expectations do you place on yourself?

___

___

___

5. How do you feel when you are abiding in the pain?

_____

_____

_____

6. How does this affect the way you respond to a triggering event?

_____

_____

_____

7. Do you feel worthy of God's love and forgiveness? Why?

_____

_____

_____

As long as I continued to live from a position of guilty, I would be self-consumed, negative, paranoid, confused, defensive, full of anxiety, reactionary, and self-conscious. I was living as defeated and I never had a chance. Satan plays on these wounded emotions and fights to make you believe them as true. He wants you to feel that you don't deserve the blessings of God. A child of God may feel these things at times, but it is no longer who you are; the feelings don't define you.

> As long as I continued to live from a position of guilty, I would be self-consumed, negative, paranoid, confused, defensive, full of anxiety, reactionary, self-conscious...just to name a few.

How will you respond to your next trigger...as a wounded child or a child of God?

Day 5: Abiding in the Vine

"I am the vine; you are the branches. If a man remains in me and I in him, he will bear much fruit; apart from me you can do nothing."
John 15:5

In John 15:5, the Amplified Bible uses the word "abide" instead of remain. "Meno" is the Greek word for abide. It means not to depart, to remain as one (Blue). Jesus wants you to be one with Him. Jesus, the Savior of the world, wants you to be part of Him so He can produce fruit in your life.

1. What does it mean to you to remain in Jesus?

   _____
   _____
   _____

2. When Jesus is the vine (when you abide in Jesus) what fruit will you bear? (Refer to Day 2, Galatians 5:22-23)

   _____
   _____
   _____

3. When your food stronghold is the vine (i.e., when you abide in your food stronghold) what fruit will be produced (i.e., strife, depression, anxiety…)?

   _____
   _____
   _____

> **You can rest in God and let Him work because He takes your burden.**

When you are rooted in Jesus, you will remain strong and confident to fight the fight that is waging inside of you, and you will reap the benefits of living in the Spirit. This is your only choice if you desire freedom. You can rest in God and let Him work because He takes your burden. Whatever you accomplish on your own will only produce temporary results. The only long-term results are those found in the Lord Jesus.

A tree reflects its root system. A weak root system produces a weak tree, and a sturdy root system produces a strong tree.

4. According to Jeremiah 17:5-6, what are the characteristics of someone who depends on the flesh and turns away from the Lord?

_____

_____

_____

5. What are the characteristics of someone who trusts in the Lord? (Jeremiah 17:7-8)

_____

_____

_____

God provides the sources—His Holy Spirit and His Son, Jesus Christ. As you plug into this power and remain in the true vine you will reap a harvest of freedom.

Food for Thought

"People all around us are having identity crises. They are trying to find out who they are. They go for therapy to discover their inner selves; they search for their roots; they try to build their sense of self-worth on the foundation of their achievements. But far more important than any of these ways of finding out who we are, we need to experience the great gift of God the Father, the gift of His Spirit who tells us that we are children of God our Father. This experience of our identity before God is not necessarily a sensational or emotional experience. It is simply an experience of the Spirit's inner witness as we pray from our hearts to God" (Intervarsity).

"Our greatest inheritance is not the abundance of things the Father gives us, but the character of His Son which the Spirit of His Son is forming within us" (Intervarsity).

Memory Verse

"I am the vine; you are the branches. If a man remains in me and I in him, he will bear much fruit; apart from me you can do nothing."
John 15:5

Closing Prayer

Dear Lord, Thank You for providing the ultimate solution for my freedom. Thank You for the gifts of Your Son and the Holy Spirit. Help me to daily trust in You and draw from these sources. I thank You that I have been made perfect because Your Son covers me. You see Jesus when you see me. He covers it all. Help me to live in these truths so I am set free to fly above the strongholds in my life. In Jesus' name I pray.

Flying Forward

- Memorize John 15:5
- **The Marble Jar**

Begin focusing on the positive things in your life...who you are and what you do. Get a container and some marbles, or other small objects, and place them in your kitchen. Put a marble in the container for every time you: do not go to the food stronghold; go to the Lord; respond as a child of God; say something positive about yourself; eat a healthy meal; take care of yourself; face a fear in your life; do any positive behavior.

Use your imagination and begin to celebrate yourself by focusing on the positives, and watch the jar fill up.

- Read through next week's study and complete each day's questions throughout the week.

Week 9

Falling Backwards

"You were taught, with regard to your former way of life, to put off your old self, which is being corrupted by its deceitful desires; to be made new in the attitude of your minds; to put on the new self, created to be like God in true righteousness and holiness."
Ephesians 4:22-24

Opening Prayer

Dear Lord, Help me to fly over the walls that I have constructed so high and so thick with so much condemnation. Demolish this wall, so I will run forward into Your arms, instead of running backwards into the arms of my man-made fortresses. Give me the strength to fly. When I feel like crawling back to those things that bring me pain, strengthen me in Your power and help me to soar over all. I can fly because You are sovereign. You are almighty. You are in control. In Jesus' name I pray.

Truth

I am a new creation in Christ and my old self has been crucified.

> I am a new creation in Christ and my old self has been crucified.

Day 1: Moving Forward in God's Forgiveness

Just One More Time

Are you ever shocked about how you feel after you run to the food stronghold, again and again? Do you ever think that it will produce different results? I would keep running back to the food behaviors, "just one more time," expecting different results. The results were always the same—start with relief (because of the numbing affect), followed by guilt, shame, remorse, self-loathing—which would then start the cycle again. I never was the winner when focused on practicing the eating behavior. It just always seemed easier to go backwards.

1. How many times have you said, "Just this one time" or "I will start tomorrow"?

   _____

   _____

   _____

2. What are your thoughts and how do you react after you have fallen backwards, (i.e., "blew" it, tricked yourself into the stronghold)?

   _____

   _____

   _____

Oswald Chambers wrote:

"Not only must our relationship to God be right, but the outward expression of that relationship must also be right. Ultimately, God will allow nothing to escape; every detail of our lives is under His scrutiny. God will bring us back in countless ways to the same point over and over again. And He never tires of bringing us back to that one point until we learn the lesson, because His purpose is to produce the finished product. It may be a problem arising from our impulsive nature, but again and again, with the most persistent patience, God has brought us back to that one particular point. Or the problem may be our idle and wandering thinking, or our independent nature and self-interest. Through this process, God is trying to impress upon us the one thing that is not entirely right in our lives"(My Utmost for His Highest, July 31).

3. What do you think God is trying to teach you every time you are faced with the same trigger over and over again?

_____

_____

_____

4. What is God trying to reveal to you at that moment of choice?

_____

_____

_____

The movie *Groundhog Day* reminds me of when I was constantly faced with the same triggers, over and over again, and I would react in the same unhealthy manner. In the movie, the main character relives the same day over and over again until he gets it right. His character was being changed as he changed his response the next time he was faced with the same circumstance. He was able to clean shop in his life. Unfortunately, we don't get the opportunity of reliving each day until we get it right, but what we do get is the freedom to choose the right choice when faced with the same circumstances. When we constantly get knocked down, when there is no hope to continue on, God is right there with His grace, His forgiveness, to prod us on to make the right choice.

What is getting in the way of making the right choice? Just as the character in *Groundhog Day* was holding onto other behaviors, I discovered that I had other coping mechanisms in my life that were feeding the food stronghold. These behaviors kept me stuck. They were roadblocks in my recovery. I had to take inventory and crucify those things that were blocking me from living as a new creation. God provides His Word and when you follow what He says you get a new start, a new beginning. Why wait for a new day to "get it right." Begin in the moment and make the right choice.

> Unfortunately, we don't get the opportunity of reliving each day until we get it right, but what we do get is the freedom to choose the right choice when faced with the same circumstances.

> I had to take inventory and crucify those things that were blocking me from living as a new creation.

5. How does it feel to fall backwards and depend on the behaviors of the past?

   _____

   _____

   _____

6. Are you aware of any habits in your life, which are producing a roadblock in your recovery?

   _____

   _____

   _____

Remember, every second is an opportunity to make the right choice. See your days as 1440 minutes. Each minute is a new day, a new opportunity to make the right choice. Don't lose the joy of today because of a mistake. We will never get it perfect; that is why we have a Father who forgives and offers us grace. You are not after perfection in your recovery. You are after freedom and healing in Christ. I had to accept Christ's forgiveness in order for me to change my "bad" day into a good one. If I overate and felt full, I would beat myself up all day. I would know in my head that I was forgiven, but how was I to live out the day feeling so uncomfortable? I would dwell on the feeling and not allow myself to enjoy today, and wishing for tomorrow to come so I could start all over. The problem lay in the fact that I couldn't forgive myself. I would beat myself up with thoughts of, *I should have known better; why did I do that again, I feel horrible.*

7. How do you handle the rest of your day after you have made a poor choice?

   _____

   _____

   _____

I did not like how I felt after I overate. I was uncomfortable. In the past, this full feeling is what would throw me into the purge cycle. I used the bulimia as a way to make myself feel better, and if I felt better, then I could start over. That just meant that every time I would fall I would have to purge, and that was my only choice. When I turned it over to Christ at that moment, my day changed. The problem was that I truly didn't accept Jesus' forgiveness and I was still striving for the "perfect" day. I had the perfect day all outlined in my head, so my day would be filled with those expectations. I was defeated even before my feet touched the ground in the morning.

> I did not like how I felt after I overate. I was uncomfortable.

8. What does Jesus offer to you that gives you a new start? (1 John 1:9)

_____

_____

_____

Day 2: A New Creation

1. According to Romans 6:6-7, what happened to your old self? What have you been freed from?

_____

_____

_____

Scripture had told me that I was now a new creation. A child's book, *The Hungry Caterpillar*, describes the transformation of a caterpillar into a butterfly. I pictured myself as a caterpillar (old self) before I accepted Christ, and as a butterfly after I became saved. It baffled me how a caterpillar changes into a totally different creature. It goes from crawling to flying, from legs to wings. A butterfly can never be a caterpillar again. I realized that I was still crawling through life, when I should have been flying. A butterfly

> A butterfly can never be a caterpillar again. I realized that I was still crawling through life, when I should have been flying.

is supposed to fly and not crawl. It would only be crawling if it was dying. So why did I continue to live as a caterpillar, when I was alive now in the Lord? He gave me a new life. He nailed my old life on a cross. It is gone. The Joni of the past is gone and dead, which meant my coping mechanisms and behaviors were dead also. Why did I constantly keep going back?

The Bible says that, *"if anyone is in Christ, He is a new creation; the old has gone, the new has come"* (2 Corinthians 5:17)! The New Living Translation describes this beautifully. "What this means is that those who become Christians become new persons. They are not the same anymore, for the old life is gone. A new life has begun!"

2. Do you "believe" you are a new creation?

   _____
   _____
   _____

3. How do you "feel" like a new creation?

   _____
   _____
   _____

4. Is most of your day spent living like a caterpillar or a butterfly?

   _____
   _____
   _____

5. Have you surrendered or crucified your old self completely to the Lord? Explain.

   _____
   _____
   _____

The hungry caterpillar chose to get out of the cocoon. It would have taken him more energy to try to stay in the cocoon than to just allow nature to perform its miracle. It takes more energy to manage a food stronghold than it takes to allow God to manage your life. Do you feel stuck in your cocoon? What is keeping you inside?

> **Do you feel stuck in your cocoon? What is keeping you inside?**

6. What is blocking the door to your cocoon?

_____

_____

_____

7. What would it look like for you to live as a butterfly?

_____

_____

_____

Day 3: Put Off; Put On

Some triggers will always be there...the people, the circumstances. How do you continue to make healthy choices if the triggers are always there? Are you able to live and walk in faith while you are still being triggered? Hebrews 12:1 tells us to "...*throw off everything that hinders and the sin that so easily entangles....*" I learned through my recovery that I was still holding on to other coping mechanisms that would feed the food stronghold I was running to.

> **Some triggers will always be there... the people, the circumstances.**

The word hinder means, "to get in the way of, to delay or obstruct the development or progress of somebody or something" (Encarta). I picture someone running a race, with weights chained around their legs, which is hindering their run. What is hindering you in your pursuit of freedom?

1. What are you to do with those things that "hinder" your life? (Hebrews 12:1-3)

   _____

   _____

   _____

2. What do you need to "throw off"?

   _____

   _____

   _____

> **The food stronghold you practice has served as a form of protection. It is a bandage over a wound that will not heal.**

The food stronghold you practice has served as a form of protection. It is a bandage over a wound that will not heal. As you begin to put a face on the stronghold, and label the triggers, the bandage will be removed. The cut is still there, but this is the beginning of the healing process. Through this process God will be revealing to you other behaviors and roots which fuel the behavior. After the bulimia ceased in my life, I was opened to other areas of my life which required healing. It is like the unpeeling of an onion. The skin of the onion is the food stronghold. Beneath the skin are different layers of the onion. As you surrender the behavior, you will begin to identify the feelings, emotions, idols, and other strongholds in your life that have been feeding the food stronghold. These were parts of my old self, the parts on which I also depended instead of depending on God.

Read Ephesians 4:22-30 and answer the following questions:

3. According to the above scripture, what are you to do with your "old self"?

   _____

   _____

   _____

4. As a new creation, in what ways can you respond to a trigger?

_____

_____

_____

The First Bite: Getting to the other Habits that Fuel the Behavior

I had to take inventory of my habits. I had to look at the place where the first seed of temptation to practice my behavior began—the precursor, what behavior or thought would begin the process. I had so many. Much was learned as I looked over the food diary to find a pattern. One of my habits from childhood was "picking." The picking was a part of me my whole life. I used picking as a coping mechanism for fear, anxiety, everything. If I wasn't picking food, I was picking my fingers and toes until they bled. When there was nothing else to pick, I would run to the food and the binge purge cycle would begin. I didn't want to get rid of the picking. It soothed me, I needed it. It was at this place, when I would start picking (temptation) that I needed Christ's strength to overcome the picking, the precursor to the bulimic behavior.

> I had to take inventory of my habits. I had to look at the place where the first seed of temptation to practice my behavior began

What happens after the process starts? What is the first bite? Is it food, yelling, picking, nail biting—what behavior starts the destructive, numbing process? It is at this point, the "first" bite, when you are to run to the cross and ask God, "What is going on Lord? Where am I hurting? What am I trying to feed or starve? Please come and show me the wound and heal it".

5. Fill in the sections of the caterpillar, on page 144, with those habits, sinful patterns, strongholds, coping mechanisms (perfectionism, worry, obsessive compulsive behavior, anxiety...) currently in your life.

6. How does it feel that you are to "put off" the coping mechanisms in your life that have been a part of you for so long?

_____

_____

_____

7. What are you to "put on"?

_____

_____

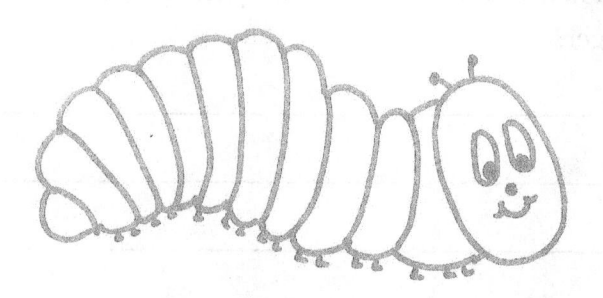

_____

8. Fill in the following blank, with those things that make up your old self (use your answers from the caterpillar in question #5). Repeat this statement for each one. Receive and believe it!

_____ is no longer my nature. I am a new creation in Christ.

Start living this very moment as your new self…because you are. You do not need your old-self coping mechanisms. If this is hard for you to believe, ask Christ to make this a reality to you.

Day 4: Satan's Tactics

> **Do you keep picking up what doesn't work? Do you find yourself returning to those behaviors that do not fill, and only lead to emptiness?**

Do you keep picking up what doesn't work? Do you find yourself returning to those behaviors that do not fill, and only lead to emptiness? Through my recovery, I would test my old behaviors. Deceived by the enemy, I was lead to believe that my coping mechanisms could provide for me what I was searching for. The food behavior did give me something tangible, something to place all my emotions onto, but in the end I would always come up empty. I felt as if I was trying to open up a door using the wrong key. I knew that I had the wrong key but I still thought maybe it would work this time.

1. Read James 1:22-25. What causes one to be deceived?

   _____

   _____

   _____

2. How do you deceive yourself into the practicing of the eating behavior? Is there anything that you do or do not do that gives you permission to run to your stronghold?

   _____

   _____

   _____

3. According to 2 Corinthians 11:3, what causes you to go back to what doesn't work?

   _____

   _____

   _____

I held the key, God's Word, and yet I would choose to not follow His Word. Partial obedience is disobedience. Satan steers you from the truths in God's Word. I held onto some of the old parts of Joni because that was what was familiar. God wants me to fly every day. He was lifting up my wings, but I was resisting. What was I afraid of, when God offers freedom, peace, joy, and love? Why not take all that, why do I settle for

> **Partial obedience is disobedience.**

less, do I feel I do not deserve it? I don't deserve it, but God wants to give it to me anyway.

4. What happens if you keep going back to the strongholds in you life (Galatians 4:9)? Describe how you have felt like a slave to the food stronghold.

   _____

   _____

   _____

5. Do you believe you are free to live without your familiar coping mechanisms? Explain.

   _____

   _____

   _____

6. What thoughts are you believing which are keeping you stuck in the behavior?

   _____

   _____

   _____

> **I have no more excuses since I am in Christ. I continued to hurt myself every time I chose to go back to a food stronghold.**

I have no more excuses since I am in Christ. I continued to hurt myself every time I chose to go back to a food stronghold. That old nature was crucified. Jesus said that I was a new creation; therefore I did not have to practice the behaviors anymore in order to survive. Jesus gave me everything that I needed to overcome. I had to make the choice to believe and put off all the negative thoughts that satan was feeding me.

Take heart. Jesus is right around the corner to conquer all satan's tactics. Don't let the "lies" make you weary. There is always a guarantee with Jesus. Jesus holds the key.

7. Read James 1:22-25. What do you need to do in order to protect yourself from falling backwards?

_____

_____

_____

Day 5: Perseverance Through the Pain

Are you searching for a pain free life?

In James 1:2, the words "whenever you face trials", shows that trials and the pain associated with them are unavoidable in this life...yet we are able "to consider it pure joy" because God uses them. I tried avoiding pain my whole life, and I thought I could by hiding in the bulimia, in the food. I was able to control the pain, leaving no room for other pain. Jesus experienced pain and faced it head on. Was I bigger than Jesus and expected more? We are to follow His example in how He "coped." The combination of my acceptance of the enemy's lies and being tired of "fighting" the same battle was the cause of my falling backwards and losing hope. Daily living out the truth of Hebrews 12:1-3 filled me with hope and put me back on track.

> I tried avoiding pain my whole life, and I thought I could by hiding in the bulimia, in the food.

Read Hebrews 12:1-3 and answer the following questions.

1. What do you need to do in order to run the race? How are you to run the race?

_____

_____

_____

Perseverance is being obedient when not feeling like it—when you can't see beyond the trees and when you have lost all hope. It is in believing what you cannot see and focusing on the eternal rewards (2 Corinthians 4:18).

Perseverance: Finding joy while carrying your cross. Hope in the darkest moments.

2. According to Hebrews 12:2, what are you to fix your eyes on? What happens when your eyes are focused on a triggering event or person, or the food stronghold?

   _____

   _____

3. What was it like for Jesus to approach His crucifixion? What made Him "endure" (bear hardship, to experience exertion, pain, or hardship without giving up) the cross?

   _____

   _____

   _____

4. How do you feel knowing that Jesus was in pain as He faced the cross, yet did it anyway? How can that help you the next time when you are faced with the temptation to practice the food stronghold?

   _____

   _____

   _____

5. What was Jesus' destination, His focus?

   _____

   _____

   _____

Falling Backwards / 149

6. What destination are you focused on?

_____

_____

_____

Victory lies in choosing God's way. I think about Jesus carrying the cross to His crucifixion. I can't image the pain. Jesus could have in one second chosen to get out of that situation. While He possessed the power, He still chose God's way. At times when I come face to face with a triggering event, which I have no power over, the pain overwhelms me. We all have a major choice in that moment—the what seems to be the easier choice, the quick fix solution of succumbing to the pressure and reacting (which always leads to unrest), or choosing to face the pain and focus on God and His way. Actually, God is the real quick fix and He is the more accessible one. Feeling the pain—again. Hurting—again. Picking up that same cross—again. Some things may never go away. Some people in your life may never change. Fixing your eyes on Jesus is the only way.

> **Victory lies in choosing God's way. I think about Jesus carrying the cross to His crucifixion. I can't image the pain.**

7. When have you felt like giving up?

_____

_____

_____

8. How do you feel today about where you are in the recovery process?

_____

_____

_____

> There were days in this process of recovery when I wanted to give up.

There were days in this process of recovery when I wanted to give up. Days filled with pain as I faced issues. I was so weary to go on, yet I needed to choose to rest in the Lord, and wait for Him. *"Wait for the Lord; be strong and take heart and wait for the Lord"* (Psalm 27:14).

He fills and gives the strength that one needs. I am able to say, with confidence, that when you are weary, when you think you can't go on, wait for the Lord, persevere in the process, do what it takes to be strong, and you will see His goodness and your burden will be lifted. As the Bible says, *"Let us not become weary in doing good, for at the proper time we will reap a harvest if we do not give up* (Galatians 6:9).

Food for Thought

"You might ask, 'What if I fail?' Satan wants you to wallow in self-pity, but don't do it! Instead, immediately ask God to forgive you. Then turn around, walk away, and don't look back. Thank God for His forgiveness, and also thank Him for the victory He is going to give you the next time you are tempted" (Stanley, "Gaining…", 9).

Memory Verse

"You were taught, with regard to your former way of life, to put off your old self, which is being corrupted by its deceitful desires; to be made new in the attitude of your minds; to put on the new self, created to be like God in true righteousness and holiness."
Ephesians 4:22-24

Closing Prayer

Dear Lord, Thank You that I am able to run to You instead of a food stronghold or any other coping mechanism in my life. Help me to persevere through the pain when I am faced with the temptation to make an unhealthy choice. Thank You that you bore the pain on the cross and that you are aware of the pain that I may experience. You hold the prize. Help me to fix my eyes on You, the Creator of all, the Creator of my destiny. In Jesus' name I pray.

Flying Forward

- Memorize Ephesians 4:22-25
- Ask yourself the following questions when you feel you are losing hope:
    - Are you isolating yourself? (Keep your support systems, reach out, don't wait for others to reach in, ask for help when needed, don't wait to be rescued)
    - Are you running from God? (check to see how big HE is in your life)
    - Are you still holding on? (Be obedient even if you don't know the "whys"—blind faith, trusting even when you don't feel like it)
    - Are you playing tricks with your stronghold?
    - Are you avoiding those things that trigger you?
    - Are you putting on the armor?
    - Are you giving yourself grace through the process?
    - Are you being honest with God? Do you believe you are free, or that you can be free?
    - Are you being fed by the Lord?
    - Are you accepting God's love and forgiveness?
- Read through next week's study and complete each day's questions throughout the week.

Week 10
Moving Forward: Flying Wounded Above

> *"There is no fear in love. But perfect love drives out fear, because fear has to do with punishment. The one who fears is not made perfect in love."*
> 1 John 4:18

Opening Prayer

Dear Lord, I give to You all my fears of the past, present, and future. Fill me with Your perfect love so that I am able to move forward. In Jesus' name I pray.

Truth

God's perfect love buries the fears of the past, present, and future.

Day 1: Facing the Waves with Confidence

> God's perfect love buries the fears of the past, present, and future.

My fear of the ocean began when I was a child. A wave had knocked me under the water, tossing and turning me around so I couldn't get up. From that point on I feared the waves. I would get my feet wet, but as soon as I saw a wave come, I would run to shore. This was also true of my life. When I feared anything or anyone, I would run in the other direction... to food and to the other "strongholds." Running away is no longer an option.

Today, I love the ocean. It is the one place that brings me peace. I no longer fear the waves. I had to face the waves, while still afraid, in order to get over the fear I had of them. In facing them, I learned how to handle them so I would not get knocked down.

Fear...I have lived my life in fear. Fear of not being pretty or thin enough. Fear of not being accepted. Fear of being judged. Fear of being yelled at. Fear of hurting someone's feelings. Fear of rejection. Fear of waiting for the other shoe to fall. Fear of myself. I thought that I had a handle on this fear. I could control it. I could keep fear at arms distance. I controlled fear by anxiety, worry, and worst of all, by bulimia.

You have to face your fears, in order for you to move on from the food stronghold. You can find what you fear in your triggers. When I feared to be alone, and was left alone—I would eat. When I feared making a decision—I would eat. It was these fears that I had to face with God, and once I did, they were no longer triggers.

You don't have to fear those triggers in your life that bring pain. God has overcome. He has conquered the power of fear in your life. You are His. Today, you can approach the "waves" with confidence, not with your confidence, but with the confidence you have in the Lord Jesus, who will provide you with everything you need in every situation and circumstance that you will face.

> Fear...I have lived my life in fear. Fear of not being pretty or thin enough. Fear of not being accepted. Fear of being judged. Fear of being yelled at. Fear of hurting someone's feelings. Fear of rejection. Fear of waiting for the other shoe to fall. Fear of myself.

1. What are the "waves" in your life that you fear? Are you willing to face them afraid?

   _____

   _____

   _____

2. Why don't you have to fear according to Isaiah 43:18-19? What are you supposed to do?

   _____

   _____

   _____

3. What do you seem to dwell on?

___

___

___

"Forget the former things; do not dwell on the past. See, I am doing a new thing!" Isaiah 43:18-19

> **Dwelling on the past inhibits you from facing the future.**

Dwelling on the past inhibits you from facing the future. Isn't the future, the unknowns of tomorrow, and the "what ifs"—that we fear? The past encompasses anything that happens from this second back to the day you were born. I could be mad at myself for days over something that I ate, or when I slipped and fell backwards into the bulimia. That constitutes the past as much as a memory from when I was a child. Focusing on yesterday, keeps you from getting on with your life. Life is made up of a series of goodbyes—but the goodbyes are always followed by a hello—hello to new growth, hello to new opportunities. Cry at your goodbyes, embrace your hellos.

4. What do you need to say goodbye to from your past that triggers you into the eating behavior?

___

___

___

5. What can you now welcome into your life?

___

___

___

Face the fear of loneliness—with God. Face the fear of rejection—with God.

Face the fear of _____ —with God.

Day 2: God's Perfect Love Conquers All

I was free. I knew that "the truth set me free", yet I continued to live in bondage. I continued to build a cocoon around me. I felt like a butterfly, in a cocoon, unable to fly. The cocoon became my armor, my shield. God was my armor and shield, yet I continued to create my own for my protection. Fear trapped me inside.

We all fear something...too scared to be thin, too scared to be fat, too scared to feel...just too scared to be...you. Fear paralyzes us, yet protects us. It is our enemy, yet our friend. I kept running away in fear, and in need to hide somewhere, so I ran to food. The anxiety of dealing with the food put me over the edge into bulimia. Fear and anxiety were able to rule in my house.

"Fear and bondage go hand in hand. The addict is afraid he will never change, fearful of what it would be like if he did change, worried about losing what he treasures most, fearful of what others think and most afraid of the dreadful crisis that every addict believes he is relentlessly moving toward" (Anderson, 122-123).

> "Fear and bondage go hand in hand."

1. List the fears from the above passage. Which fears are true to you? Explain.

   _____
   _____
   _____

2. Do you fear losing weight? Do you fear gaining weight? Why? What fears about approaching food do you have?

   _____
   _____
   _____

Fear keeps you in bondage to the past, in bondage to failure, in bondage to unbelief. Fear doubts what God says is true. Fear is behind all negative behaviors. I ate because I feared—I feared rejection, failure, loneliness, weight gain—everything. Fear builds a cocoon of isolation, paranoia, anxiety, and worry around you. But the truth says that perfect love drives out fear.

3. How did God express His "perfect love" towards you?

_____

_____

_____

> **There is no need to punish yourself by running to a food stronghold that puts you in bondage.**

God loves you with a perfect love. A love that has promised you a life in eternity with Him. God loves you perfectly, just as you are. You are able to trust Him with everything because of His great love for you. This perfect love drives out fear. There is no need to punish yourself by running to a food stronghold that puts you in bondage. Run to the Lord—because of His great love and because He can be trusted. Jesus bore your sins on the cross, and He carries your burdens. Your freedom lies in Jesus. Jesus has taken care of your past, present, and future, therefore giving you the freedom to fly.

4. How does the truth that your future is sealed in Christ, with His perfect love, help you to not fear the future? How does it help you to face life without your food stronghold?

_____

_____

_____

Peace is a restful state of trust. Without peace there is anxiety, and anxiety is caused by a fear of the unknown.

5. What causes anxiety in your life? How does God tell you to combat anxiety in Philippians 4:6-7?

_____

_____

_____

6. Where are you to place your anxiety according to 1 Peter 5:7? What is the opposite of anxiety?

_____

_____

_____

7. According to John 14:27, Jesus gives us peace. How does having Jesus' peace help you with your fears?

_____

_____

_____

Be not afraid. God's gift of peace covers all. Anxiety fuels the behavior, but when resting in Him, you no longer have to fear. He is your shield, so you no longer have to create your own.

"I sought the Lord, and he answered me; he delivered me from all my fears." (Psalm 34:4)

> "I sought the Lord, and he answered me; he delivered me from all my fears." (Psalm 34:4)

Day 3: Press On

You are free to fly—finally—because you are allowed to. God tells you that you are free. God tells you not to be in bondage to the past and to move on. That is the only way you will be able to fly. You no longer have to fear. You are allowed to live in peace, allowed to be joyful, allowed not to be anxious or fearful—just because God said so.

> You are free to fly—finally—because you are allowed to. God tells you that you are free.

Carrying the past around, past hurts, past mistakes, past behaviors, is bondage.

1. What parts of the past do you still carry around? What are you looking for when you look back?

   _____

   _____

   _____

Genesis 19 tells of the destruction of Sodom and Gomorrah. God had saved Lot and his family from the destruction, by telling them to flee. He warned them though in Genesis 19:17 to not look back. Genesis 19:25-26 tells us, *"But Lot's wife looked back, and she became a pillar of salt."*

2. What did Lot's wife do in verse 26? What happened? Why do you think she looked back?

   _____

   _____

   _____

It was as if Lot's wife was "frozen" in the past. She looked back because she feared the unknown of tomorrow.

3. How do you stay frozen in the past? (dwelling on it, wanting it to change, looking for answers, changing it, denial, doubting your adoption, bringing it with you, unable to let go)

   _____

   _____

   _____

Moving Forward: Flying Wounded Above / 159

4. What is the main lie of the past that fuels your behavior?

_____

_____

_____

Picking up the past will never fill the empty places that only Jesus needs to fill. I kept carrying around my old self. Every time I chose to "look back", it led to my own destruction.
Read Philippians 3:12-14 and answer the following.

5. Does Paul (the author of this book) claim to be perfect? What action does he take as he remains in his "imperfect" state in verse 12?

_____

_____

_____

6. What two steps go hand in hand? (vs.13)

_____

_____

_____

7. Why should you strain and press on?

_____

_____

_____

8. What "prize" do you receive when you are focused on the food stronghold? What happens when you focus on your past hurts or your behavior?

_____

_____

_____

> It is time to bury the past and move on and follow Christ.

Forgetting your old habits of reliance and then "straining on" takes effort. Your eating behavior has been a part of you and it is familiar. Give yourself grace as you embrace your new lifestyle, learning to live as a new creation.

It is time to bury the past and move on and follow Christ. Accept the past as the past, grieve through the hurts, and have Jesus heal the wounds. Jesus says in Luke 9:62, *"No one who puts his hand to the plow and looks back is fit for service in the kingdom of God."* Whenever I look back in pursuit to change what already has taken place, my peace and joy are stolen. I become focused on the regrets, bitterness, and the anger—which bring them into the present, and clog any hope for the future. They become baggage. You take on more weight, which will continue to feed the eating behavior, which can lead to falling back to those unhealthy patterns. Release the weight to Jesus; give Him your past, everything about it—so you can become weightless.

I know this is hard, but believe me it is worth the pain of letting go. The joy of the Lord that you will experience is worth the race. My stubbornness, rebellion, and my disbelief kept me in defeat.

Day 4: The Armor of God

> When you face the future with God, you need not fear.

When you face the future with God, you need not fear. Fear led me to food, and then fear kept me from flying. Fear is of satan, not of God. 2 Timothy 1:7 says, *"For God has not given us a spirit of fear, but of power and of love and of a sound mind"* (NKJV).

1. What is fear associated with, according to 1 John 4:18?

_____

_____

_____

Anorexia, bulimia, and compulsive overeating are all a form of self-inflicted punishment.

2. Do you feel a need to punish yourself or a fear of being punished?

_____

_____

_____

I always felt that I had to punish myself for my thoughts, emotions, temperament, and my flaws. The starving, compulsive overeating, and purging were all a form of punishment. Even after the behaviors stopped, I still continued to listen to the lie that I deserved to be punished.

3. What lies are fueling the belief that you need to hold on to the past?

_____

_____

_____

Satan says that you can't move on because of your past, and God says you can move on in spite of your past. God tells us how we are to fight satan. He gives us tools in Ephesians 6:10-18 (Refer to this scripture when answering the following questions).

> **Satan says that you can't move on because of your past, and God says you can move on in spite of your past**

162 / Weightless: Flying Free

4. What happens when you put the armor on? (vs.13)

_____

_____

_____

5. List the parts of the armor and their purpose?

_____

_____

_____

6. Which pieces would help you most in your fight against a food stronghold?

_____

_____

_____

> **Daily putting the armor on is like putting sunscreen on as protection against the sun's damaging rays.**

Daily putting the armor on is like putting sunscreen on as protection against the sun's damaging rays. God's armor protects you against the evil one and the temptations that you daily face. The enemy will use anything and anyone to bring you down. Since you are no longer a slave to your past, you do not have to live as a victim. Satan tries to bring your mind back to what you have lost, but you have to press forward to look ahead to what Jesus has for you. It is more than enough. You don't have to fear because you are sealed into the family of God.

Day 5: Denying Self

1. Are you willing to take the risk to lose everything you cling to for Jesus? Explain.

_____

_____

_____

2. Would you forfeit your soul, your joy, for the sake of _____? (Fill in the blank with the things, people, and circumstances, you are waiting to see change before you can enjoy)

_____

_____

_____

I have allowed my past wounds to infect my present. I was holding onto the past because I didn't believe that I could move forward and be free to live, unless I received items from my demand list (people's approval, perfect weight and size,...). As I focused on the unmet needs of the past, I would relive the pain, and my only option was to numb the pain with food. Now that I am a child of God, I can go immediately to Christ and He alleviates the pain, He loves me, He accepts me—just as I am. Food became the "middle man." Now I go directly to the supplier for all my needs and I can walk with joy and peace.

> Now that I am a child of God, I can go immediately to Christ and He alleviates the pain, He loves me, He accepts me—just as I am.

Refer to Mark 8:34-35 to answer the following.

3. What are the three steps you must do when you "come" after Him?

_____

_____

_____

4. What does it mean to you to:

- deny yourself?

_____

_____

_____

- take up your cross?

- follow Jesus?

5. What is your cross?

Following Jesus requires self-denial, complete dedication and willing obedience.

6. What do you personally have to deny yourself daily (within your control) in order to help you have a day free from a food stronghold? What do you need to let go of that is out of your control?

Reflect on Hebrews 5:7-9 and answer the following.

7. Did Jesus give up in His struggles?

8. What did He do when He was suffering? What did He learn from His suffering?

_____

_____

_____

Jesus had to "learn" obedience. Knowing that Jesus had to learn something, and He is God's Son, why do I think that I shouldn't have to go through anything? Until you persevere through a trial, with God, not succumbing to temptation, you will never know what obedience feels like. Once you overcome a temptation, overcome reacting to a trigger, and taste freedom, you will crave that success.

The funny thing is that when I was bulimic I was living a life of denial, and now in order to be free, I am told to "deny" myself. I had to deny my past, deny my rights for how I think people should act, deny my wanting anything more that what God has provided for me today, and to deny my old self and everything that was associated with it. Walking in God's perfect love conquers all the fear in order for you to move forward to fly wounded above.

> The funny thing is that when I was bulimic I was living a life of denial, and now in order to be free, I am told to "deny" myself.

Food for Thought

A Conversation with God

Me: I want food. I just don't care anymore.

God: Why don't you care anymore?

Me: Because I feel that no one else does.

God: But I do.

Me: But that isn't enough.

God: Why am I not enough?

Me: I want certain people here on earth to care.

God: But this isn't your real home.

Me: I want heaven on earth right now, I am tired of waiting.

God: Trust me! I know what is best for you and I love you. You have to let it all go. It is in the letting go of everything that you are clinging to in this world–your wants, your desires, and your past–that will set you free. Follow Me. Rejoice in your freedom, rejoice in your new self, and rejoice just because you are my child.

Deny yourself and let God be God, so He can become your everything.

Memory Verse

"There is no fear in love. But perfect love drives out fear, because fear has to do with punishment. The one who fears is not made perfect in love."
1 John 4:18

Closing Prayer

Dear Lord, Thank You for giving me the strength to fly. You have given me wings, which are being held up by You. Lord, continue to help me to fly over all the "stuff" that is bringing me down. Help me to soar over all. When I feel like I want to crawl back to those things that bring me pain, strengthen me in Your power and help me to soar over all. I can fly because You are Sovereign. You are Almighty. You are in control. In Jesus' name I pray.

Flying Forward

- Memorize 1 John 4:18
- Read through next week's study and complete each day's questions throughout the week.

Week 11

Weightless: Flying Free

"And we know that in all things God works for the good of those who love him, who have been called according to his purpose."
Romans 8:28

"For I know the plans I have for you," declares the Lord, "plans to prosper you and not to harm you, plans to give you hope and a future."
Jeremiah 29:11

Opening Prayer

Dear Lord, thank You for piecing me back together, according to Your plans. Help me to be patient in this process as You weave my life together for good. In Jesus' name I pray.

Truth

I am God's perfect package designed to fly free.

> I am God's perfect package designed to fly free.

Day 1: True Contentment

I won't grow up until...

In a recent dream, the song from Peter Pan, "I Won't Grow Up" kept playing. The next day, I couldn't get it out of my head. I just knew that there had to be a message in it, because it was so bizarre for that song to be in my dream. I felt God wanted to tell me something. Peter Pan is described as the boy who wouldn't grow up. I have been holding on to some parts of my past that were causing me to stay as a child. I didn't want to grow up UNTIL certain things from the past and present were changed. This was so true of the bulimic years, because I kept waiting for "until", before I would stop the behavior.

The past will never change. I was fighting a losing battle. Fighting a fight that I can never win creates a bitter, angry, anxious child. I was still living as a child "stuck" in those destructive patterns—UNTIL—**until** I lose weight, **until** I make more money, **until** she/he changes, **until** I hear the words "I love you and "I am sorry", **until** I figure it all out, **until** I don't hurt anymore....

I felt like a pauper walking around begging for someone to fill the empty spot in my heart, a spot that I didn't surrender to Jesus. Jesus wants us to live our lives despite the "untils". Some will come, some won't. I get older year after year, waiting for the day that "I can grow up". As long as I held on to the past, I could be an 80-year-old child, still waiting.

When Jesus came into my life, He gave me a new life, a new past. My past is His. He has redeemed it. He is the UNTIL. It wasn't UNTIL Jesus came into my life that I was able to fully grow up. Jesus became enough for me. Just as Peter Pan's Wendy couldn't fly until she believed, I couldn't fly until I believed.

> When Jesus came into my life, He gave me a new life, a new past. My past is His. He has redeemed it.

1. What are some of the "untils" in your life that are keeping you stuck in your stronghold?

   _____
   _____
   _____

2. Do you believe Jesus is enough to replace those "untils"?

   _____
   _____
   _____

Life is about right now. Focusing on the fears of the future, the pain of the present, or the end result, robs you of today's joys. God's love must become enough for right now, no matter how you are feeling, no matter what you desire—His love is enough for you to live your life despite the untils.

3. Have you wondered, "When will this go away" so I can begin to live my life? What feelings are associated with that question?

_____

_____

_____

Paul "...*learned to be content in all circumstances*"(Philippians 4:12). Contentment doesn't mean being satisfied with the end result. It means being okay with where you are today, where you were yesterday, while not worrying about tomorrow. Content in knowing that whatever happens is okay because it is in God's control.

> **Contentment doesn't mean being satisfied with the end result. It means being okay with where you are today,**

4. What did Paul say was the secret to contentment in Philippians 4:13?

_____

_____

_____

5. How is Jesus' strength enough for you to be content today?

_____

_____

_____

6. How does Romans 12:12 help you to be content as you go through the recovery process? In what ways does your contentment affect the desire to practice a food behavior?

_____

_____

_____

You can live today *"joyful in hope, patient in affliction, and faithful in prayer"* (Romans 12:12), because of the strength that you receive through Jesus Christ. You don't have to focus on "when will this be over" anymore. It is actually over now, with Christ. The journey is just beginning. You are allowed to enjoy Jesus and just sit back and enjoy the ride even though it may feel uncomfortable. Feeling unfamiliar does not make something wrong. Changes, which are beneficial to your life, will feel uncomfortable. Isaiah 64:8 tells you that God is the potter and you are the clay, the work of His hand. Every day, God is forming you. At times I picture myself on the potter's wheel and God has made me a cup, and then I get smashed and He starts forming me into something else. When I fight the process, it hurts. I have to laugh now, even when it does hurt, because it is just part of God's process of molding me.

> I have to laugh now, even when it does hurt, because it is just part of God's process of molding me.

It is really about God's plan, not yours. It is about God's timeline, not yours. His plan looks different than yours, yet is the right one, so why not trust Him in the process. Since He has an answer for every stumbling block in the process, you can live today in freedom even while dealing with the unresolved issues of your life. Don't wait until you "arrive" to be joyful. Fly high today while reaching for the prize found in Christ.

Day 2: Pieced Together

You don't have to live as a wounded child any longer. You are allowed to move beyond the feelings and "untils". You are free to fly beyond the stronghold, because God has promised to restore *"....all the years the locusts have eaten..."* (Joel 2:25). Job lost everything in his struggle, and God blessed him 100 times more. God promises that whatever you have lost or whatever you have given up, He will restore 100 times more (according to the plan He has for your life) and store up treasure for you in heaven (Matthew 19:21).

> You don't have to live as a wounded child any longer.

The Bible describes this in the book of Joel. Famine and locusts destroyed the land of Judah. The Lord offered the people a solution.

Refer to Joel 2:12-13, 25 to answer the following questions.

Weightless: Flying Free / 171

1. What does God tell the people of Judah to do?

   _____

   _____

   _____

2. How is God described? Is this a God who you can trust?

   _____

   _____

   _____

3. What promise does God give to those who repent in verse 25?

   _____

   _____

   _____

4. How can this passage help you with the "untils" in your life?

   _____

   _____

   _____

Your life is made up of the past, present, and future. It is like three puzzles. Each puzzle is made up of the "all things" that God talks about. Each piece represents a person, circumstance, and place.... The puzzle of your past has already been put together. God takes those pieces and uses them in the present to work good in your life. According to Romans 8:28-29, when you turn those over to Him, He will use all the pain of your past for the good of your todays and tomorrows.

> **The puzzle of your past has already been put together. God takes those pieces and uses them in the present to work good in your life.**

5. What are the puzzle pieces of your life that are being used for good? (Romans 8:28)

   _____
   _____
   _____

6. What are some of the puzzle pieces of your life that you have given to God? Which pieces do you still hold in your hand?

   _____
   _____
   _____

7. What "good" have you seen come from some of those past pieces? How does that make you feel?

   _____
   _____
   _____

Day 3: Blessings from the Battle

> God has turned my battle with food strongholds into good; into so many rich blessings. It was worth the fight.

God has turned my battle with food strongholds into good; into so many rich blessings. It was worth the fight. God has blessed me beyond what I could ever imagine. My battle with bulimia may be over, but I have seen so much good come from it. This battle brought me to my knees and in return I received the precious gift of Jesus. I believe that if I never suffered, I would have never found or needed my Lord. The opportunity to share His glory, His love, His power, and His hope, with all of you is a blessing beyond words.

God will always use everything that you place on His altar. God is real, even if you can't feel Him. God is real, even if you don't think you are making progress. Everything you are going through, God knows about. There are no surprises with God. You weren't a surprise. Your trials aren't a surprise to God. Your reading this book is not a surprise. Nothing is by accident with God. God placed me, and God placed you in the family that He did for His purpose. God placed you right where you are right now for His purpose. All the pieces of the puzzle will begin to make sense to you.

1. How do you feel that God will work all things together, even your food stronghold, for good?

   _____

   _____

   _____

2. Jeremiah 29:11 tells of the plans that God has for your life. What are they? How does that help you to continue living in the present?

   _____

   _____

   _____

Christ has redeemed your past. Christ has redeemed all those years that the locusts have eaten. As you move forward in trust, your wounds will be healed, and you will reap the blessings. It takes a step forward to move beyond what is left behind.

Read the account of Peter walking on water in Matthew 14:25-31 and answer the following questions.

3. When did Peter decide to get out of the boat?

   _____
   _____
   _____

4. When did Peter become afraid (vs.30)? What was he focused on and what happened?

   _____
   _____
   _____

5. According to verse 31, why did Peter fall? What will keep Peter afloat?

   _____
   _____
   _____

6. What are you to focus on, to keep you from sinking?

   _____
   _____
   _____

7. What is the outcome when you remain focused on the Lord?

   _____
   _____
   _____

> **You don't have to go back to the past, or fear the past because you have been set free—forever.**

You don't have to go back to the past, or fear the past because you have been set free—forever. God has provided everything you need for today, and whatever you will need in the future. Jesus has taken care of your past, present, and future, which gives you the freedom to fly—unafraid.

Day 4: You are The Perfect Package

My recovery process has been a time of self-discovery. I continue to be in process, a life process, of God's changing me. As I surrender myself to God, He reveals areas in my life that I need to change. I have learned a lot about Joni, the Joni that God has constructed. I have learned to value my body and myself because it is God's.

You are the perfect package...you are God's child, His workmanship, redeemed by His Son, filled with the Holy Spirit, and your body is considered a temple. You are a precious package that deserves the proper care. You are free to celebrate yourself.

> **You are a precious package that deserves the proper care. You are free to celebrate yourself.**

1. What does 1 Corinthians 6:19-20 call your body and how are you supposed to care for it?

   _____

   _____

   _____

2. What are the first words that come to mind when you hear the word "temple"? What kind of care does a temple deserve?

   _____

   _____

   _____

3. How does it make you feel that your body is a temple?

   _____

   _____

   _____

4. How do you view your body knowing that it is the temple of the Holy Spirit?

_____

_____

_____

> **Temples come in all different styles and designs.**

Temples come in all different styles and designs. No matter what it looks like, it is still a temple, a place where God resides. God's children, likewise, are all different sizes and shapes, and unique. You are a temple and that deserves a celebration.

5. The Bible tells us in to honor God with our body in I Corinthians 6:20 and "...*whether you eat or drink or whatever you do, do it all for the glory of God*" (1 Corinthians 10:31). How can you apply these truths to your life?

_____

_____

_____

6. Take inventory of your habits (sleep, fun, rest, eating...). What does your body need for peak performance?

_____

_____

_____

Honoring your body doesn't mean honoring the perfect size or weight. It means caring for yourself because you matter to God. Through all my dieting days I had been slowly mistreating my body, in subtle ways; abusing a good thing, my body, that the Lord has created and has given me the responsibility to care for. Over indulgence or starving your body strips you of the joy that the Lord wants you to have. I housed the Holy Spirit of our Lord, and I still chose to vandalize it. I would never vandalize a church, yet I did it to my own temple. Your body is a machine. It needs proper nourishment in order to run. A car is fueled by gas, so you would never fill the tank with water. Why do we play around with our bodies? If you begin with the mindset that "food is for fuel" and eat for those reasons, you will begin to treat yourself better. As you begin to grow in your relationship with the Lord, and follow His principles, you will want to honor God in whatever you do.

Day 5: Life is Good, Because God Is!

Life is not a burden. It is the burden that you add to your life that makes it one. It is not a burden to take care of yourself. The world's standard of "the sky is the limit" in all areas of your life – physically, mentally, financially, and spiritually– has made it a chore. Shooting for the expectations of the world does become a burden. It is fun to care for yourself in the way God has intended. It is hard to start if you are not used to it. The choices are unbelievable. It is all about your focus. Focus on the world and a food stronghold is only a distraction. A distraction needs a new focus.

> **It is fun to care for yourself in the way God has intended. It is hard to start if you are not used to it.**

1. What does God tell you to focus on in Philippians 4:8? How would that change your outlook of how you perceive yourself and your circumstances?

   _____

   _____

   _____

2. What are those things in your life that are praiseworthy and excellent?

   _____

   _____

   _____

3. Who has God placed in your life that has been a blessing? What are her/his attributes? What can you learn from this person?

_____
_____
_____

A clothing line has the saying "Do what you like. Like what you do" (Life). I never really knew what I liked to do because all my time was spent managing my eating and the bulimia. I also didn't feel that I deserved to enjoy, doing what I wanted to do. I had to experiment and try things. I felt like a kid in a candy store, overwhelmed and not knowing what to choose. Look into your heart and ask God to reveal to you the real you. Discover yourself. Treat yourself. Enjoy putting this piece of the puzzle together.

> **Look into your heart and ask God to reveal to you the real you.**

4. Take time to consider the following questions:

- What brings you joy?

    _____
    _____
    _____

- What do you like to do? Where do you like to go?

    _____
    _____
    _____

- What makes you smile?

    _____
    _____
    _____

- What makes you laugh? What makes you cry?
  _____
  _____
  _____

- If you could do anything, what would it be?
  _____
  _____
  _____

- What do you like to do on a sunny day? On a rainy day?
  _____
  _____
  _____

- In what areas do you excel?
  _____
  _____
  _____

- How do you relax?
  _____
  _____
  _____

- What is your favorite exercise?
  _____
  _____
  _____

- What is your favorite food?
  _____
  _____
  _____

- Who are you?

_____

_____

_____

There is freedom in just being you—filled with your likes and your dislikes. This is where freedom begins...with nothing to hide. I observed people on the beach. Everyone is in a bathing suit, and every body type is represented. No one is hiding behind his or her clothes. Everyone is equal. The mask is off. They are free to be themselves, because they have to. Their hearts are exposed. Once uncovered, with nowhere to hide, the fear is gone and they are able to be themselves.

They no longer have to hide, ashamed, like Adam and Eve in the garden before sin entered. They were totally free to enjoy their life. Once sin entered, they hid their bodies in fear. When focused on the world and stuck in sin patterns (hiding), you can't be the person God made you to be.

> It is pretty funny how now I find enjoyment in most of the things in which I used to fear and in what would trigger me into the behavior.

It is pretty funny how now I find enjoyment in most of the things in which I used to fear and in what would trigger me into the behavior. Begin to try those things, which you fear, and it may be in those where you find joy. I feared God, and He is my ultimate place of joy. Find what works for you. Have fun discovering yourself. Every time that you choose not to run to a food stronghold you are opening up another part of the real you that God wants to fill. The sky is the limit...but only with the Lord. So fly in His sky.

Food for Thought

"As you've struggled with your eating disorder, most of your time has been spent just surviving. Now that you've begun your journey toward health and wholeness, you can start to think about living again.... As you put all the puzzles of the past into place, you can accept yourself, discover new energy, and relearn how to live" (Jantz, 141).

Memory Verses

"And we know that in all things God works for the good of those who love him, who have been called according to his purpose."
Romans 8:28

"For I know the plans I have for you," declares the Lord, "plans to prosper you and not to harm you, plans to give you hope and a future."
Jeremiah 29:11

Closing Prayer

Dear Lord, Thank You for piecing my life together for good. Thank You for making me a perfect package, designed to bring glory to Your name. Thank You for restoring my past life into a future secured in the loving arms of Your Son. In Jesus' name I pray.

Flying Forward

- Memorize Romans 8:28 and Jeremiah 29:11
- Read through next week's study, completing the questions.

Week 12

Perfect Peace To Soar

"The Lord is my strength and my shield; my heart trusts in him, and I am helped. My heart leaps for joy and I will give thanks to him in song."
Psalm 28:7

Opening Prayer

Dear Lord, Thank You for Your grace and Your gift of freedom. Thank You for everything that You have revealed to me through this study. Provide for me the continued support, through Your Word and other people, so I can continue on this road of freedom. In Jesus' name I pray.

Soaring

You are only able to see part of the puzzle that God is piecing together of your life. Do you trust Him with the rest of the story? What are you to do now that God has been uncovering the lies beneath the food stronghold and you are shedding the food stronghold that has been your focus?

"We live by faith, not by sight" (2 Corinthians 5:7). God is always working. He will never leave you. At times, you may not feel His presence. He has not gone anywhere; just like when the sun is hidden on a cloudy day. His "Son" will always be present in your life. He wants you to trust Him in the storm, through the clouds, and especially when you don't feel like it.

1. What truths has God revealed to you about yourself, over the last 12 weeks?

   _____

   _____

   _____

2. What growth have you experienced spiritually, emotionally, relationally, and physically, since you began this process?

   _____

   _____

   _____

3. In what areas do you still struggle?

   _____

   _____

   _____

4. How do you feel as you finish this last week?

   _____

   _____

   _____

God's perfect peace will always be available to you to get you through anything.

5. What are you told to do in Philippians 4:9? What will you receive?

   _____

   _____

   _____

6. How is peace attained in Isaiah 26:3-4?

   _____

   _____

   _____

7. How will God's peace help you as you continue through this process?

> Through all my struggles and pain, God's perfect peace surpasses all, no matter what the outcome.

Through all my struggles and pain, God's perfect peace surpasses all, no matter what the outcome. God promises His perfect peace, and when this peace is experienced, there is nothing better than His perfect peace in the storms of life. The storms may remain, but in His peace is found the stillness, the calmness, and the answer—to everything. One of my favorite scriptures is Philippians 4:6-7: *"Do not be anxious about anything, but in everything, by prayer and petition, with thanksgiving, present your requests to God. And the peace of God, which transcends all understanding, will guard your hearts and your minds in Christ Jesus."* I have experienced this peace, which transcends all understanding. I depend on this peace for everything.

8. How can you be joyful as you continue this path to healing? (Psalm 28:7)

> My joy is no longer found in a pant size, a number on a scale, or in the search for a perfect day.

Joy can only be found in the good that is to come, not in what used to be. My joy is no longer found in a pant size, a number on a scale, or in the search for a perfect day. My joy is found in the Lord, the producer of joy. He has already used my pain and turned it into joy. I think about what I would be like today if I never took the step to go after my Lord. He is always present, He is always all-powerful, and He is always sovereign. Rest is found in your Savior's arms. Rest is found in a relationship with God. Rest is found in living as God's child. He will never leave you. He is the Great I Am. He is faithful, even when you are not. He forgives your sins, over and over again. He loves you—just as you are, and all that He asks is for "you"—all of you, so He can lavish His love on you, just because you are accepted, you are loved, you are forgiven. May God's love, God's grace, and His Son Jesus, "WOW" you as you rest in His arms and allow Him to just love you as you are—just because He wants to.

9. What steps do you need to take in order to continue on your journey of freedom?

_____

_____

_____

10. How can the people that God has brought into your life support and encourage you?

_____

_____

_____

11. "Be still" before the Lord, and write a prayer. Thank Him for this journey, what He has done in your heart, and for what He will continue to do in your life. Share your heartfelt needs.

_____

_____

_____

God will continue to reveal the beautiful story of the life He has planned for you, as you continue to make God the main character. This is only part of my story. I don't know what God will do with the rest of the pieces, but I do know the ending—"she lived happily ever after" with Jesus, and I pray that this is the ending of your story.

Food for Thought

Daily evaluate your progress in the following:

Steps for Success

1. Fall in love with God
   - Daily spend time in the Bible
   - Pray
   - Journal
2. Take your focus off of the food...remember that it is not about the food
3. Label your triggers
4. Give yourself grace
5. Embrace the recovery process...be patient with yourself
6. Surround yourself with "safe" people...those people who encourage you and love you for just being you
7. Get involved in a group, church, and Bible study
8. Minimize the food stronghold. It is not who you are
9. Throw off those things that are stumbling blocks
10. Give the Lord your broken heart and ask Him to heal your wounds
11. Believe that the Lord will heal you
12. Live today as if you were free...because you are in Christ!

Memory Verse

"The Lord is my strength and my shield; my heart trusts in him, and I am helped. My heart leaps for joy and I will give thanks to him in song."
Psalm 28:7

Closing Prayer

Thank You Lord that…
You have chosen me…just because
You have accepted me…just because
You love me…just because
You offer your forgiveness…just because
You protect me…just because
You provide all my needs…just because
You offer your peace and joy…just because
You rejoice over me with singing…just because
You wipe my tears…just because
You will never leave me…just because
You have turned every hurt into good…just because
You have healed my wounds…just because
You have given me a second chance…just because
Just because…You are God

Flying Forward

- Memorize Psalm 28:7
- Ask God to provide the means to help you continue to grow spiritually
- Meditate on God's truths that speak to the areas of your life where you are attacked spiritually

Appendix A: Food Diary

Time	Behavior	Event/Circumstance	Emotions/Mood "I feel..." "I am..."	Food Eaten or denied

Appendix B: Additional Resources/Support

BIBLE STUDIES

Freedom From Addiction Workbook by Neil T. Anderson and Mike & Julia Quarles
Conquering Eating Disorders Workbook (12 Step), by Robert S. McGee & Wm. Mountcastle
Breaking Free: Making Liberty in Christ a Reality in Life Workbook by Beth Moore
Living Free Workbook by Beth Moore
Overcoming Negative Self-Image by Neil T. Anderson and Dave Park

BOOKS

Life Stories

Bulimia

The Monster Within by Cynthia Rowland McClure

Anorexia

Starving For Attention by Cherry Boone O'Neil (True story of an Anorexic's battle and triumph)

Weight and Self-Image

The Inner Beauty Series by Lisa Bevere
You Are Not What You Weigh, Out of Control and Loving it, The True Measure of a Woman, Look Beyond What You See, Give Up and Get Free, Discover Your Inner Beauty

Comfortable in Your Own Skin: Making Peace with Your Body Image by Deborah Newman

Anorexia, Bulimia, Overeaters

Hope, Help, & Healing For Eating Disorders by Gregory L. Jantz, PhD

The Thin Disguise by Vredevelt, Newman, Beverly, & Minirth

Love Hunger: Recovery from Food Addiction by Minirth & Meier

Counseling Those with Eating Disorders by Raymond E. Vath, M.D.

Other Issues

Addiction and Grace by Gerald May, M.D.
Healing for Damaged Emotions by David Seamands

WEBSITES

Remuda Ranch: http://remudaranch.com
National Eating Disorder Association: http://www.nationaleatingdisorders.org
National Association of Anorexia Nervosa and Associated Disorders: http://www.anad.org
CaringonLine: http://www.caringonline.com/
The Center for Counseling and Health Resources, Inc.: http://www.aplaceofhope.com/eating.html

ORGANIZATIONS

American Anorexia/Bulimia Association (AA/BA)
165 West 46th Street, Suite 1108
New York, NY 10036
(212) 575-6200

Eating Disorders Resource Center (EDRC)
24 E. 12th St., Suite 505
New York, NY 10003
(212) 989-3987

American Anorexia/Bulimia Association (AA/BA)
293 Central Park West, Suite 1 R
New York, NY 10024
(212) 501-8351

Something Fishy
1104 Smithtown Ave., Suite 121
Bohemia, NY 11716

National Association of Anorexia Nervosa and Assoc. Disorders (ANAD)
PO Box 7
Highland Park, IL 60035
(847) 831-3438

References

Anderson, Neil and Mike and Julia Quarles. *Freedom from Addiction*. U.S.A.: Gospel Light Publications, 1997.

ANRED: Anorexia Nervosa and Related Eating Disorders, Inc. "Statistics: How many people have eating disorders?" http://www.anred.com/stats.html. November, 2005.

Blue Letter Bible. "Dictionary and Word Search for *'meno (Strong's 3306)* ' ". <http://www.blueletterbible.org/cgi-bin/words.pl?word=3306&page=1>.1996-2002. November 2005.

Boone, Cherry. *Starving for Attention*. New York: Dell Publishing Co., Inc., 1982.

Campus Crusade for Christ. "Four Spiritual Laws." http://www.crusade.org/downloads/article/resources/4SpiritualLaws.pdf . October 2005.

Carle, Eric. *The Hungry Caterpillar*. New York: Philomel Books, 1987.

Carlson, Nancy. *I Like Me*. New York: Puffin Books, 1988.

Celebrate Recovery. "Do you Suffer from an Eating Disorder." http://www.celebrate-recovery.org/Groups/Eating/CR%20Eating%20Inventory.pdf. Accessed September 17, 2012.

Chambers, Oswald. *My Utmost for His Highest*. Uhrichsville: Discovery House Publishers, 1992.

Claude-Pierre, Peggy. "The Secret Language of Eating Disorders." http://www.randomhouse.com/features/eatingdisorders/stats.html. Nov., 2005.

Concerned Counseling Eating Disorders (C.C.E.D.). "Eating Disorders Definitions." http://www.healthyplace.com/Communities/eatingdisorders/concernedcounseling/definitions.htm. 2000.

Eldredge, John. *Waking the Dead*. Nashville: Thomas Nelson, Inc., 2003.

Encarta Dictionary, Microsoft online.

Evans, Darrell. "Trading My Sorrows." Integrity's Hosanna! Music. 1998.

Gillham, Anabel. *Building up and the tearing down of Strongholds (tape series)*. Fort Worth: Lifetime Guarantee Ministries.

Helming, Brent. "Your Beloved." Mercy/Vineyard Publishing: 1996.

Intervarsity Press. " Moving from Slavery to Freedom." IVP New Testament Commentary. http://www.biblegateway.

com/resources/commentaries/index.php?action=getCommentaryText&cid=7&source=1.%201995-2005.&seq=i.55.4.1. 1995-2005.

Jantz, Gregory L. *Hope, Help, & Healing For Eating Disorders.* Wheaton: Harold Shaw Publishers, 1995.

Life is good clothing retailers

Liimatta, Michael. "Theology of Christian Recovery" adapted from "A Guide to Effective Rescue Mission Recovery Programs." http://www.alcoholicsvictorious.org/theology.html. 1993.

Matthew Henry Commentary on the Whole Bible (1706-1721). Book of Joel, chapter 2, verses 12-13. http://www.ccel.org/h/henry/mhc2/MHC00000.HTM.

McClure, Cynthia Rowland. *The Monster Within.* Grand Rapids: Fleming H. Revell, 1984-2000.

Merriam-Webster Dictionary online, http://www.m-w.com/cgi-bin/dictionary.

Moore, Beth. *Living Free.* Nashville: LifeWay Press, 2001.

Mosser, Jonell and Pierce Pettis. "You Did That For Me." *All Right Here.* Universal-Polygram International Publishing Inc.: 2002.

Meyer, Joyce. *Beauty From Ashes.* USA: Warner Faith, 1994-2003.

Meyers, Ruth. *31 Days Of Praise.* Sisters: Multnomah Publishers, Inc., 1994.

Moneypenny, John. "God's Love For Us." http://www.gospelfortoday.org/jteachings/godslove.htm. 2001-2005.

Ramis, Harold, Director, *Groundhog Day,* 1994.

Remuda, *Beyond the Looking Glass.* Nashville: Thomas Nelson, Inc., 1992.

Stanley, Charles. *Finding Peace.* Nashville: Thomas Nelson, Inc., 2003.

Stanley, Charles. "How To Handle Our Burdens." *Intouch Magazine.* July, 2005.

Stanley, Charles. "Gaining Victory Over Temptation." *Intouch Magazine.* Sept., 2004.

Stanton, Andrew. Director, *Finding Nemo,* 2003.

Vath M.D., Raymond E. *Counseling Those With Eating Disorders.* Dallas: World Publishing, 1986.

Wimmer, Carol. "When I Say that I am a Christian". http://carolwimmer.com/when-i-say-i-am-a-christian. 1988.

CPSIA information can be obtained
at www.ICGtesting.com
Printed in the USA
JSHW060351140123
36047JS00001B/4

9 781490 8981